William Henry Wahl

The Franklin Institute Of The State Of Pennsylvania

William Henry Wahl

The Franklin Institute Of The State Of Pennsylvania

ISBN/EAN: 9783741148064

Manufactured in Europe, USA, Canada, Australia, Japa

Cover: Foto ©Thomas Meinert / pixelio.de

Manufactured and distributed by brebook publishing software
(www.brebook.com)

William Henry Wahl

The Franklin Institute Of The State Of Pennsylvania

THE

FRANKLIN INSTITUTE

OF THE STATE OF PENNSYLVANIA FOR THE
PROMOTION OF THE MECHANIC ARTS.

A SKETCH

OF ITS

ORGANIZATION AND HISTORY

COMPILED BY

WILLIAM H. WAHL

SECRETARY OF THE INSTITUTE

PUBLISHED BY THE INSTITUTE

PHILADELPHIA

1895

The Franklin Institute.

The objects of the Franklin Institute, which has just closed the seventieth year of a useful and honorable career, are defined in the Act of Incorporation (March 30, 1824) to be " the Promotion and Encouragement of Manufactures and the Mechanic and Useful Arts."

It was the first institution of its class to be established in the United States, and, though embodying in the scheme of its organization, many of the features of the so-called " Mechanics' Institutes," its scope was more broadly gauged, and its working methods constructed on a higher plane, than these. It was, if the comparison be permissible, the result of a compromise. Neither the Mechanics' Institutes, which sprung into existence like mushrooms about the time when the organization of the Franklin Institute was being considered—and which were devoted almost wholly to the instruction of artisans by means of lectures and classes—nor the exclusive societies of those learned in the sciences and arts, answered to the ideas and needs of the founders. An instrumentality was sought through which these two elements, so diverse in character, yet potentially capable of being mutually so helpful, could be brought into fraternal relations—a platform was needed, broad enough and strong enough to accommodate professor and layman, master and workman, side by side, without incommoding either ; in brief, an institution was wanted which should have inscribed on its corner-stone, " Science with Practice ; Practice with Science."

To give material form to these ideas, our institution was founded ; and the sentiment, above quoted, has been its animating spirit from the beginning to the present.

4

The founders chose for it, of all names, the most fitting
—that of the illustrious printer, statesman, philosopher—the
synonym of broad utilitarianism.

The Franklin Institute was organized in the year 1824,
chiefly through the personal efforts of Samuel V. Merrick,
who had in Prof. William H. Keating, a helpful coadjutor.
In an autograph letter of Mr. Merrick to the Hon. Frederick Fraley, some interesting reminiscences bearing on the
subject are, fortunately, preserved. From this letter, it appears
that Mr. Merrick, then a young man of twenty-one years,
found himself "the owner of a workshop, without a mechanical education, with scarcely a mechanical idea." The first
step which he took to improve this situation was a disas-
trous one.

He applied for membership in a local association
of mechanics, and, lacking the necessary qualification for
membership, was *black-balled.* This apparently trivial circumstance appears to have caused him to take into consideration a suggestion made by a friend, Mr. Wm. Kneass, to
found an organization patterned after his own ideas.

After meeting with several discouraging failures in the
attempt to interest others in such a scheme, he was induced
to visit Prof. Keating, then a young man, who had recently
been elected to a professorship of Chemistry applied to
Agriculture and the Mechanic Arts, in the University of
Pennsylvania, and who, it so happened, had also met with
discouragement in a recent effort to secure co-operation in
establishing an institution of science.

The immediate outcome of the conference between these
young enthusiasts was the issuing of a call for a preliminary
meeting of friends of their enterprise, at which plans could
be discussed and the needful preparations taken to call a
public meeting. This preliminary meeting, as Mr. Fraley
records in his interesting historical sketch, presented at the
celebration of the fiftieth anniversary of the Franklin Institute, was accordingly called. The list of those who attended,

and of those who had previously signified their willingness to aid the project, includes the names of the following persons, who are entitled to the honorable distinction of being the first promoters of the new society, viz.: Matthias W. Baldwin, Peter A. Browne, Oram Colton, Thomas Fletcher, Robert E. Griffith, Wm. H. Keating, Wm. H. Kneass, David A. Mason, Samuel V. Merrick, James Ronaldson, James Rush, George Washington Smith, M. T. Wickham and Samuel R. Wood.

At a subsequent meeting of these promoters, a plan of organization, a constitution, etc., were approved, and measures were taken to call a public meeting. To this end, a list was made of the names of some 1,500 citizens selected from the city directory, and to these an invitation was sent for a meeting to be held in the County Court-house, at Sixth and Chestnut streets. This meeting was held on the evening of February 5, 1824, and was largely attended. Mr. Merrick, in his letter to Mr. Fraley, states that "the meeting was a perfect success; and the novel mode of throwing the association open to the world, without the intervention of cliques, made it universally popular."

No contemporaneous printed record of this meeting exists, but Mr. Merrick records that it "was presided over by James Ronaldson, Esq., and after the purposes of the proposed institution had been fully explained by Col. P. A. Browne and others, an animated discussion took place until the subject was fully understood by a highly intelligent assembly, who unanimously accorded their approbation of the purpose in view. After which the constitution was presented, critically discussed, and after amendment was unanimously adopted and a day fixed for the election of officers from those who should previously enroll their names, and which numbered some three to four hundred.

" The election having taken place, the Franklin Institute assumed its position among the institutions of the State, and has since attained a gratifying pre-eminence."

Mr. Fraley's sketch gives the following additional information respecting this meeting and the proceedings incident thereon, and which resulted in the organization of the new institution :—

James Ronaldson, then the leading type-founder in the United States, was chosen to preside. Peter A. Browne, Esq., a distinguished member of the bar, stated the plan and purpose of the proposed institution and ably urged its formation; others followed. A letter of approval was read from Nicholas Biddle, then in the height of his power. The constitution was adopted. Lists of membership were circulated. A committee was appointed to nominate candidates for offices and managers, and to take the needed order for holding an election on the 16th of the same month. By the time of holding an election of officers, between four hundred and five hundred members were enrolled. Mr. Ronaldson was elected president. A board of managers was chosen, of which, as a matter of course, Mr. Merrick and Prof. Keating were members. Standing committees on instruction, on inventions, on premiums and exhibitions, on the library, and on models and minerals, were appointed and took hold of their duties with zeal and earnestness. Prof. Keating was appointed Professor of Chemistry; Prof. Robert M. Patterson, of Natural Philosophy and Mechanics, and William Strickland, Esq., of Architecture.

Officers and managers elected.

In the original draft of the constitution of the Institute, and in the charter of 1824, the objects are referred to as "the promotion and encouragement of manufactures, and the mechanic and useful arts," and as the working features of the Institute were gradually evolved within the few years immediately following its organization, the means by which these objects were to be attained eventually crystallized into the following form :—

"First, by the delivery of lectures on the arts and the application of science to them; second, by the formation of a library of books relating to science and the useful arts, and the opening of a reading room; third, by the examination of all new inventions and discoveries by a committee of learned and honorable men; fourth, by the publication of a journal to contain essays on science and art, specifications of English and American patents, etc.; fifth, by holding exhibitions of American manufactures and awarding medals to worthy workmen; sixth, by building a hall for the meetings of the Institute and the use of the members; seventh, by collecting machines, minerals, materials, etc., used in the mechanic arts; eighth, by the establishment of schools in which should be taught architecture and *mechanical drawing*, chemistry applied to the arts, mechanics, and, if possible, of a high school for giving young men a liberal and practical course of education."

On March 3, 1824, the Legislature of the State of Pennsylvania granted the society a charter, under the title " An act to incorporate the Franklin Institute of the State of Pennsylvania for the Promotion of the Mechanic Arts," which was the final act in the work of organization.

In the following pages the operations of the several branches of the Institute are treated under separate chapter heads, whenever it has been found practicable to separate them. Much information which the writer has thought to be sufficiently interesting or important to place on record, is introduced incidently, and, it is hoped, will be found interesting to those who, in after years, may glance through these pages.

Mr. Ronaldson continued to act as president until the year 1841, when Samuel V. Merrick succeeded him. Mr. Merrick held the office until 1854, and was followed by John C. Cresson, who in turn served until 1863.

In 1864, on the accession of William Sellers to the presidency of the Institute, as Mr. Fraley records, " the plan of organization was modified, and a large sum was raised by Mr. Sellers and his friends to reduce the debt, to repair and alter the hall, and to bring the institution into more effectual contact with manufacturers and mechanics." The Secretary was made a salaried resident officer, elected annually, given

8

executive functions and charged with duties of a scientific and literary nature.

The changes thus brought about were of a substantial nature, and benefited the Institute in many ways. More interest was interjected into the meetings (held on the third Wednesday of each month, except in July and August), at which papers on important scientific and technical subjects were read and discussed, new inventions were exhibited and described, and a report on current matters of interest in science and the useful arts was presented by the Secretary; and a general revival of interest and activity in all departments of the Institute took place.

Presidents. Mr. Sellers was succeeded in office, in 1868, by J. Vaughan Merrick, the eldest son of the founder. His successors, in order of service, have been : Dr. Coleman Sellers (1870–1874), Dr. Robert E. Rogers (1875–1878), Wm. P. Tatham (1879–1885), Col. Chas. H. Banes (1886), Joseph M. Wilson (1887–   ).

Secretaries. Prior to the year 1864, the office of secretary was an honorary one, and was filled by the following gentlemen, in the order named : Frederick Fraley, Prof. Alexander Dallas Bache, Chas. B. Trego, J. B. Garrigues and Prof. John F. Frazer. Since reorganization in 1864, the Secretaries have been: Dr. Henry Morton (1864–1869), Dr. William H. Wahl (1870–1874), Jacob B. Knight (1875–1878), Dr. Isaac Norris (1878–1881), Dr. William H. Wahl (1882–   ).

Actuaries. The responsible office of actuary, to which are relegated the business affairs of the Institute, has been occupied by William Hamilton (1828–1871), D. Shepard Holman (1871–1885), Herbert L. Heyl (1885–   ).

In the following, are defined the conditions, terms and privileges of membership :—

Classes of members. The members of the Institute are divided into the following classes, viz.: Contributing Members, Stockholders, Life Members, Permanent Members and Non-resident Members.

Any person of legal age, friendly to the mechanic arts, is eligible to membership in the Institute. It is necessary, however, to be proposed by a member in good standing, and to be elected by the Board of Managers. The candidate may, at his (or her) option decide to become a contributor or a stockholder. Contributing members pay eight dollars each year. The payment of one hundred dollars in any one year secures life membership, with exemption from annual dues.

Second-class stock, of the par value of ten dollars, is subject to an annual tax of six dollars per share, and entitles the holder of one share to the privileges of membership.

Each contributing member and adult holder of second-class stock, when not in arrears for dues, is entitled to attend and take part in the meetings of the Institute, to use the library and reading room, to vote at the annual election for officers, to receive tickets to the lectures for himself and lady, and to receive one copy of the Journal free of charge, and additional copies at the rate of three dollars each per year.

Minor children, wards and apprentices of members not in arrears, by payment of two dollars, have the use of the library and reading room and admission to lectures; or, admission to the lectures only, for one dollar.

Minor holders of a share of second-class stock, by paying three dollars per year, have the use of library and reading room, and admission to lectures.

The Board of Managers has authority to grant to any one who shall in any one year contribute to the Institute the sum of one thousand dollars, a permanent membership, which may be transferred by will or otherwise.

Newly-elected members, residing permanently at a distance of fifty miles or more from Philadelphia, may be enrolled as non-resident members, and are required to pay an entrance fee of five dollars and two dollars annually. Contributing members, if eligible, on making request therefor, may be transferred to the non-resident class by vote of the Board of Managers, and are required to pay two dollars annually.

Members in good standing have the privilege of introducing strangers to the meetings, and of obtaining a limited number of tickets for lectures for distribution among friends. Non-resident visitors, on proper introduction by a member, are accorded the privileges of the Institute for a limited period.

The old hall. The hall of the Institute, a plain and substantial struction of marble, stands on the east side of Seventh street, between Market and Chestnut streets. It was built from plans furnished by John Haviland, architect. The corner-stone, we are told by our venerable historian, was laid " with appropriate Masonic and other ceremonies, on the eighth day of June, 1825, at noon." The funds for the purchase of the lot and the erection of the building were provided by the issue of a building loan, which was freely taken by members and friends of the enterprise, and has since been repaid dollar for dollar. The building was completed, and the Institute took possession of all except the second floor (which was occupied by the United States Courts until 1830), in 1826. Upon the first floor are located the lecture-room (capable of accommoding about 300), and preparation rooms. The second floor is occupied by the library, to which special attention is paid elsewhere. The third floor is given up entirely to the use of the large drawing classes, composed of young men and women pursuing studies in mechanical, architectural and free-hand drawing.

The rapid growth of the library and schools of the Institute, of late years, has taxed the ingenuity of its officers to the utmost to carry on its work effectively, the accumulation of books, models, instruments, etc., having become so great as to make it almost imperative to secure more ample quarters.

Mr. Fraley's historical sketch makes allusion to the fact that the Institute, sixty years ago, had already begun to feel

the need for a more commodious building, as the following
quotations will show:—

" This dear old hall is associated with so many pleasant
and useful memories, that whenever removal to a new building has been agitated, it has given rise to strong emotions.

" But it has so happened that the intention of removal Removal plan-
ned in 1836.
has several times been seriously considered. It very nearly
culminated in the year 1836, when the Masonic Hall property
on Chestnut street, west of Seventh street, was purchased
by the Institute for the sum of $110,500.

" Plans for a new and enlarged hall were prepared by
William Strickland, Esq., architect, aided by a committee of
the Institute. A plan for a building loan was adopted, and a
part of it subscribed for, which enabled the Institute to pay the
first installment of the purchase money. But the great
financial crash of May, 1837, struck our project down, and
after vainly struggling for several years to carry it out, we
had at last to surrender it, and at a fearful loss of many
thousands of dollars. At different times since, projects of
removal have been started, but, grown wise by the experience
of 1837, we have not been again tempted into any uncertain
contracts."

The reference to the failure of the Institute to realize its
plan in 1837, might properly have contained the additional
information that the financial loss thereby entailed, severely
crippled the resources of the Institute for a number of years
thereafter.

In order to promote and encourage, on the part of its Sections or de-
partments.
large membership, a more general participation in active
scientific and technical work, the Institute lately approved
a plan, carefully drawn and matured by the managers, by
which the members of the Institute are divided into departments or sections representing various branches of science
and the arts, each section having control of its own domestic affairs, but all subordinate to the general authority of the
Institute.

Under the previously existing order of things it was felt that the direction of the scientific and technical work of the society was left too largely in the hands of the secretary and the Committee on Instruction, with the inevitable result that of the nearly 2,000 persons comprising the membership, a comparatively small proportion only took an active part in its work. The change above referred to, it is anticipated, by affording the members enlarged opportunities for personal action, will supply the needed stimulus to induce many who hitherto have held aloof, from diffidence or want of encouragement, to take the initiative and engage actively in the cultivation of special branches of pure and applied science. The successful realization of these anticipations will greatly broaden the field of usefulness of the Institute. The Chemical Section and the Electrical Section, both useful and active bodies of several years' standing, have already felt the influence of this change by a considerable increase of membership. The organization of other sections will proceed as rapidly as circumstances will justify their formation.

Creation of a Board of Trustees, 1887. In 1887, the Institute took the important step of creating a Board of Trustees, vested with ample authority to receive and hold for the benefit of the society all the real and personal estate of the Institute which should thereafter be acquired by subscription, or devise, bequest, or donation. The property acquired since this action was taken—and which in the aggregate amounts at present to about $40,000—and all that may hereafter be acquired, save where the donors shall expressly provide to the contrary, passes at once into the custody of the trustees, who are required to hold it in trust for the purposes specifically designated by the donors, or, where there is no specific designation, for the benefit of the Institute.

The act of the Institute creating the trustees, specifically directs the officers of the Institute forthwith to convey to the Board of Trustees, all property received by them. The act further gives the trustees authority to perpetuate their existence, by filling vacancies which may occur in their body. In this procedure, the Board of Managers of the Institute is given the right of selecting the successor of a trustee from three suitable persons nominated for the office by the remaining members of the Board of Trustees.

By these (and other confirmatory) provisions, it will be perceived that all property acquired since the creation of the trustees, or which may hereafter be acquired, by subscription, bequest or otherwise, becomes forthwith vested in the Board of Trustees, and cannot in any event be liable for any debts which the Institute may possibly contract. Friends of the Franklin Institute, accordingly, who may contemplate making it the beneficiary of their bounty, thus have the fullest assurance that the terms of a subscription, or the directions of a bequest, will be literally and faithfully executed in perpetuity. *All property acquired vested in the trustees.*

No one feature of the Franklin Institute so fully demonstrates the sincerity of its devotion to the objects for which it was organized—the promotion of manufactures and the mechanic and useful arts—as the democratic character which has always been its distinguishing mark. *A democratic body.*

Its membership is open to men and women, without regard to distinctions of race, nationality or religion, the only requirements for admission being good character and friendly interest in its work. The artisan and the professor meet within its walls upon an equal footing, animated by the single desire to increase the common stock of knowledge by mutual contributions, and to this fortunate blending of " science with practice," which is so pre-eminently exemplified by the life-work of the illustrious Franklin, much of the usefulness, past and present, of the Institute, should be ascribed.

This is happily expressed by President Sellers in his address at the fiftieth anniversary celebration of the Institute. After alluding to the organization of great numbers of Mechanics' Institutes in England and Scotland, about the time when our own Institute was being formed, and to the fact that, with few exceptions, these enterprises enjoyed only a brief period of active usefulness and then languished and died, he gives the explanation in the following words :—

"Our Franklin Institute was from the beginning a Mechanics' Institute, in one sense of the word. It taught by lectures and sometimes by classes, but it was always more than was contemplated by the societies abroad. If I may so express myself, it was and is a *democratic learned society;* it is not exclusive. No well-behaved person is excluded from its membership. All who desire to reap its benefits or to aid it in its great work of promoting the mechanic arts can join it. This is not so with the so-called learned societies of this and other lands. They select their members from among those who have already distinguished themselves in the arts or sciences, or are likely so to distinguish themselves: hence, their membership is confined solely to the learned of the land. Now, mark the difference in our case. Learned men join our society, and in its hall come in contact with those who may be unlearned so far as books are concerned, but better informed in some special art or trade. Theory and practice are brought together, and each helps the other."

Those who are most familiar with the Institute will best be able to recognize how truly this explanation explains the very source and origin of its vitality.

To all who are interested in the progress of the arts and manufactures; in the increase and diffusion of knowledge; in the training, especially of the young, by precept and example, in habits of industry and self-dependence; and in the cultivation of those things which tend to make men and women more useful to themselves and more helpful to others; the Franklin Institute opens its doors in welcome.

The roll of membership at the present time includes about two thousand names; but in Philadelphia, the very citadel of American manufactures, and with a population of

Who are eligible as members.

over a million, ten times that number should be enrolled on its list. With the moral and substantial aid which half that number would contribute, it would be enabled to accomplish in its chosen fields, in education, the promotion of the useful arts, and the encouragement of invention, vastly more and better work. Its opportunities for usefulness are almost unlimited, but it is compelled to restrict its activities in many directions for the want of money to provide the needful means and facilities.

Its usefulness restricted for want of means.

Except the meagre income derived from bequests and endowments (and which, in all, amount to some $60,000, the greater portion of which sum has only lately been acquired), the revenue upon which the Institute has always been compelled to rely for its maintenance has been derived entirely from the annual fees of its members. While its influence, directly and indirectly, in stimulating the progress of the arts and manufactures, during nearly three-quarters of a century, has gained for it a leading position among the institutions of the land, and has benefited the whole country, and while it has again and again responded to the call of the city, the State and the nation, by placing freely at their disposal the services of a trained and skillful body of experts in the arts and trades, the Franklin Institute has never received a dollar of public money for carrying on its own work.

What it has accomplished in the past has been done with limited financial resources and inadequate facilities. For years it has been hampered for want of room to provide for the increase of its library, and for want of modern equipment for its schools, its laboratories and its lecture hall. Its present building is inadequate in size, antiquated in its appointments, and in a location which is becoming year by year more unsuitable and uninviting. It is in the very midst of warehouses and manufacturing establishments, and the constant danger of destruction by fire, to which its library and other treasures are exposed, has long been the cause of grave anxiety to its managers and members.

Hampered for room.

Unsuitable and dangerous location.

It needs now, and imperatively, a new and more commodious house, fire-proof, centrally situated, and fully equipped with the most approved facilities for its work. These should include a well-lighted and properly-appointed library and reading-room, provided with every convenience for study, consultation and copying; an auditorium capable of seating comfortably 1,500 to 2,000 persons, and furnished with every modern convenience for the proper illustration of scientific lectures; laboratories for chemical, mechanical and electrical investigations, in which its committees would be able to do their work in the most convenient and effective way ; and well-appointed class rooms for its drawing school and other educational work.

A larger building needed, fire-proof and with modern equipment.

The endowment of the library, the Journal, and schools, on a basis sufficiently ample to provide for their permanent maintenance on a plane of creditable efficiency, is scarcely less imperatively needed than a new building, and must be provided in the near future.

The task of providing for these urgent needs of the Institute is now receiving the most serious consideration of the managers, and their plans, which are gradually being matured, it is hoped and believed, will merit the cordial approbation of the members, and command from them and from their public-spirited fellow-citizens in the city and State, in whose behalf the Institute has done so much good work, such substantial evidences of sympathy and support as will insure their early realization.

Then will this grand old Institute, which for nearly three-quarters of a century has worthily borne, and added lustre to, the honored name of Franklin, rejuvenated and reinvigorated, as a giant refreshed with wine, enter upon a career of renewed and extended usefulness.

With a word of testimony from others, this chapter may fittingly be brought to a close.

From the forthcoming volume on " Industrial and Art Education " in the United States, edited by Mr. J. Edwards

Clarke, published by the United States Bureau of Education, the following generous acknowledgment may appropriately be introduced at this point.

Referring to the influence exerted by the Franklin Institute, he says:

"The precedence, in time, of the founding of the Franklin Institute; its example, inciting to the establishment of similar organizations in other cities; its important direct and indirect influence upon many phases of national development, as well as upon elementary and technical education in the city of Philadelphia—witness the relations held by it, through Dr. Jones and his journal, to the national patent system and its history; the fact that the future architect of the Capitol at Washington received his first upward impulse and elementary technical training in its schools; and its claim of having been first to suggest the holding the Centennial Exhibition, as already recorded in the extracts from the Ledger article; all combine to give exceptional interest to the history of this association of mechanics.

"An Institute, which has counted among its active members men of such recognized eminence as scientists and educators as Dr. Thomas P. Jones, the founder of the Franklin Journal; Alexander Dallas Bache, who organized the 'Committee on Science,' and who left the Institute only to assume the position of Superintendent of the Coast Survey of the United States; Prof. John C. Cresson; Prof. Henry Morton, long Secretary- of the Institute, editor of the Journal, and now president of the Stevens Institute, Hoboken; Prof. Robert E. Rogers; and Prof. George F. Barker, of the University of Pennsylvania, who, in 1874, assumed the editorship of the Franklin Journal, is surely entitled to take rank in the United States among the leading institutions for the promotion of science.

"While a local institution, whose list of presidents contains such names as fill the roll of the Institute, namely, James Ronaldson, Samuel V. Merrick, (the original founder of the Institute), Prof. John C. Cresson, William Sellers, John Vaughan Merrick, Prof. Robert E. Rogers, and Coleman Sellers, needs no better indorsement in the city of Philadelphia.

"The early opening of the drawing classes of the Institute gives it precedence in the movement for the better

technical training of mechanics; while the fact that the
'School of Design for Women' was founded by it as long
ago as 1850, entitles it to consideration in any account of the
movement for the training of women in Industrial Art; these
two acts link it to the whole industrial and artistic educational movement which has, in recent years, become such a
feature in education, and has given such an impulse to industrial and artistic development in many parts of the United
States; while the initiation of the movement which culminated in the success of the Centennial Exhibition is an
instance of a direct impulse given by a local institution to
the industrial and artistic development of a whole people."

And the same author elsewhere says, in referring to the
public services of the Franklin Institute: "The work you
have done seems admirable, and an example that should be
placed before the country."

The *Public Ledger*—conservative and just in all things—
speaking of the Institute, has this to say :—

"Its achievements, we believe, have been more
thoroughly recognized and appreciated everywhere than here
in its own home. This is said to be characteristic of Philadelphia, that it does not 'exploit' its own good works. It
would be well if our people were of a different habit in this
respect, and it would be better if,   *   *   *
there should be inaugurated a new era of the recognition
and appreciation of its merits, its services, its great usefulness, and its honorable record. If Boston possessed such
an Institute, with such a history, its renown would not be
allowed to become dim at home by any lack of public pro-
clamation of what it is and what it has done."

Educational Features—
Schools, Lectures.

As part of the original scheme of the Institute contemplated the education of mechanics and others in the sciences which constitute the foundation of the trades, the first Board of Managers, elected to office February 16, 1824, and which effected the organization, provided for the establishment of a standing Committee on Instruction, charged Committee on Instruction. with the duty of directing the educational work of the Institute. This committee has been maintained to the present without substantial modification of its duties.

This committee speedily perfected plans for systematic instruction by means of lectures. Professorships of chemistry, of natural philosophy and mechanics, and of architecture, were established and filled by the election of capable instructors.

The first course of lectures, as we learn from the invaluable record preserved to the Institute in the historical sketch of Mr. Fraley, was held in the old Academy Building, on Fourth street near Arch, owned by the University of Pennsylvania, the use of which for this purpose was granted by the trustees; and it is also recorded, that the work of the professors was ably supplemented by a corps of volunteer Lecture courses and Drawing School established. lecturers from the membership of the Institute. A little later, the Institute rented the lower floor of the old Carpenters' Hall for this purpose, and finally, on the completion and occupancy of the hall, the lectures were held in its own lecture room.

The next step taken in this direction was the formation of a school for the teaching of mechanical and architectural drawing, which was effected in the year 1824. This experiment

seems to have been crowned with complete success ; and,
encouraged by the support which their efforts to provide for
the educational wants of the city received from their appreciative fellow-citizens, the managers proceeded to establish
another school, in which should be taught "all the useful
branches of English literature and the ancient and modern
languages." This project was realized in 1826. In 1827,
the records show that over three hundred scholars were upon

High School es-
tablished. its roll. It was the model upon which the Central High
School, shortly afterwards established by the city as part of
the public school system, was patterned. With the organization of the public high school, that of the Institute was
abandoned as unnecessary. The drawing school, however,
was continued, and has maintained an uninterrupted existence to the present. Its leading feature—that of training
pupils for actual work in shop and office—has always been
rigorously preserved, and at the present time, as a school
for mechanical draughtsmen, it is conceded, by those best
qualified to judge, to be the most thorough and practical of
any in the country.

The lectures also, have occupied a prominent place in
the scheme of the Institute's work, from the beginning to the
present. For many years, they were of the nature of a regular
course, or series, on architecture, mechanics, physics and
chemistry, varied of course from year to year, but following
generally the plan of graded or consecutive instruction, as in
schools and colleges. This system, however, though for a
long period admirably useful in meeting the needs of the public,
was found in time to be gradually outgrowing its usefulness.
Lecture courses on scientific themes, which for years had been
practically pre-empted by the Franklin Institute, in time,
were made attractive features in the schools and colleges,
and the popular science lecturer became a conspicuous figure
on the public lecture platform. And so it came about, naturally, that the Committee on Instruction found it advantageous
gradually to modify its plans to adapt them to the changes

of the times. For a number of years, accordingly, the character of the Institute lectures has departed widely from the old-time pattern. The object at present most conspicuously kept in view in the selection of the lectures, is to give the members of the Institute the advantage of having presented to them the latest advances in the useful arts and the sciences bearing thereon ; and, to this end, the committee's efforts each year are directed to the purpose of securing the services of men of eminence in their respective fields of labor, who are invited to select their own themes. The lecture courses, thus, are greatly varied from year to year, but the quality of the material presented, generally, is of the highest order of excellence. An inspection of the lists of lecturers announced in the programmes of the past ten years will disclose many names famous in the ranks of American science and industry, and the pages of the Journal, during this period have been enriched with a varied collection of material, presenting in a concise and interesting way the progress of all branches of science and the arts, as expounded by their ablest representatives.

Though devoted more especially to the promotion of the mechanic arts, the Institute in numerous ways has shown its sympathy with the efforts of those who have sought to elevate the standard of taste among our people by the cultivation of the fine arts as applied to the industries. Thus, the present flourishing "School of Design for Women," was founded by the Institute, June 20, 1850, and for several years was conducted by a committee assigned to this work, until it had become self-supporting ; and, to another admirable institution —the " Pennsylvania Museum and School of Industrial Art," the Institute extended its friendly co-operation, a helping hand, and a sheltering roof, during the period of its infancy. *Interest shown in industrial art.*

An interesting fragment of history, preserved in the sketch of Mr. Fraley, is worth reproducing at this point, to show the extent of its influence, even at the outset of its career, viz.:—

"The general interest created by the existence and working of the Institute caused more attention to be paid to technology and to science generally, and in the year 1837 gave rise to a movement for the establishment of a School of Arts. The Institute headed this movement and applied to the councils of the city for a grant of a large plot of ground in West Philadelphia as a site for the buildings of the proposed school.

"This was promptly and cheerfully granted, and the legislature was appealed to by memorials from all parts of the State to endow the school by a liberal appropriation."

The project, as our historian records, failed of success at the time, but has since been fully realized in the plans of the University of Pennsylvania.

Movement for a
School of Arts,
1837.

The Library.

The plan of the founders contemplated "the formation of a library of books relating to science and the useful arts, and the opening of a reading-room;" and, accordingly, one of the first steps taken in the work of organization, was the appointment of a committee charged with this duty. Committee on Library.

The founding of the Journal, in 1826, by opening the way to the establishment of exchange relations with other societies and with the leading magazines and periodicals devoted to science and the useful arts, proved an invaluable help in promoting its growth, and thus, early, gave to the library the distinctive character which it has since maintained. From the nucleus formed by this useful agency has grown a reference library of scientific literature, in some branches unique, and, in extent and completeness, second to none in the United States, embracing the publications of the principal scientific and technical societies of the world, and the leading periodicals devoted to science and the useful arts. Aided by the Journal.

In 1887, the Moyamensing Literary Institute, which, up to that time had been designated as a public depository of the United States government publications, finding that its facilities were inadequate to meet the requirements imposed by law upon libraries of this class, surrendered its claims in favor of the Franklin Institute, which has since remained the public depository for the congressional district in which it is situated. By this transfer the library also became the custodian of a large number of valuable publications, which had previously been deposited with the institution above named, and which proved of substantial assistance in contributing to the completion of sets of the publications of the various scientific and technical bureaus of the government. The library a public depository.

Among the publications of this class, of which the library at present possesses sets which are, in most instances, complete, should be named, the coast and harbor charts of the United States Coast and Geodetic Survey, and of the Hydrographic Office; the publications of the Engineering Bureaus of the Army and Navy; those of the United States Geological Survey; of the Department of Agriculture; and of the United States Patent Office.

Collection of patent records. The governments of Great Britain, (and her colonies), France and Switzerland, also, have deposited with the library, complete sets of their patent office publications, with the stipulation that they should be kept conveniently accessible to the public for reference. To make the collection of this valuable class of publications—which, collectively, constitutes an epitome of the world's progress in the arts and manufactures—as comprehensive as possible, the Committee on Library has lately acquired complete sets of the patent reports of Germany and Austro-Hungary.

Value as a library of reference. The library is annually enriched, also, by the gift of numerous technical publications of a miscellaneous character from foreign governments, and from States and municipal authorities and corporations. These embrace publications relating to public works; official reports relating to geology, the mining and metallurgical industries, agriculture, public health, municipal engineering; reports of railway and other transportation companies, manufacturing corporations, etc.

For many years it has been the policy of this committee, to increase the value of the collection as a library of reference, and to this end it has devoted systematic effort to the task of completing the files of its important serial publications. In this work, the committee, with the substantial assistance of several liberal contributions of money from generous friends of the Institute, has been notably successful.

To inventors and manufacturers seeking for information respecting the state of the arts and manufactures, the extensive collection of patent literature which the library places

at their disposal, is simply indispensable, and the library is
constantly resorted to by attorneys and their clients for the
purpose of consulting these volumes; while, to the professional man and the student, the scientific and technical
serials in which the library is so rich, are no less indispensable as an aid in pursuing their investigations.

For the acquisition, by purchase, of the standard and
current works relating to the arts and sciences, the means
which the Institute could place at the service of its Library
Committee, for many years, were extremely limited, and the
collection of books of this class increased very slowly.
Many valuable books were acquired by gift, but, for a long
time, the yearly accretions by purchase were inconsiderable.
At the close of the fiftieth year of its existence, the Institute
had on its shelves only 12,000 volumes. Since then, however, the library has received substantial aid from several
sources, and (when compared with its previous history) has
increased rapidly.

In the year 1878, through the liberality of Mrs. Bloomfield H. Moore, the Institute received the sum of $10,000
for the endowment of the library as a memorial of her
deceased husband, Bloomfield H. Moore, who, for a number
of years was greatly interested in the Institute, and especially in the work of its Library Committee, of which body
he was long an active member. **Endowment of Mrs. Moore.**

The principal of this fund was increased in the year
1888, by a second gift from Mrs. Moore, of $5,000, making
the total amount of this endowment, $15,000.

In the year 1874, the library was enriched by the deposit
therein of the valuable personal library of the late John
Lenthall, for many years Chief of the Bureau of Construction
and Repairs of the United States Navy. This deposit, which,
on the death of Mr. Lenthall in 1883, became a gift, consists
of nearly 1,000 volumes relating to naval architecture,
marine engineering and kindred subjects, included in which
are a great number of drawings. This collection, designated **Gift of the Len-thall collection**

the " Lenthall Collection," is used solely for reference, and forms a valuable addition to the literary treasures of the Institute.

" Memorial Library " of the Electrical Exhibition

In the year 1884, through the efforts of a special Committee on Bibliography, a valuable collection of literature relating to electricity was made in connection with the " International Electrical Exhibition," held under the direction of the Institute, in the autumn of that year. To this collection, publishers, authors and scientific societies, at home and abroad, made liberal contributions, and the committee's labors resulted in the acquisition of 3,000 volumes, bound and unbound, monographs and pamphlets, relating to electricity and magnetism. This library, properly classified and catalogued, formed an interesting feature of that notable exhibition. At the close of the exhibition, this collection, in accordance with the proposition contained in the invitation accepted by the donors, was deposited in the library of the Institute as the " Memorial Library of the International Electrical Exhibition," to be used for reference only. In addition to the above-named books and pamphlets, this committee received contributions of money amounting to nearly $1,000, which was invested, and the income of which is now applied to the preservation and increase of the collection.

Other benefactions.

In the list of those whose generosity has enriched the library should be mentioned, also, as especially worthy of grateful remembrance, the names of Algernon S. Roberts (1869), and Henry Seybert (1878), each of whom contributed a considerable sum of money for the purchase of standard reference books ; that of Mrs. Wm. B. Rogers (1885), who made a gift to the library of the large and important collection of works on chemistry owned by the late Dr. Robert E. Rogers, one-time President of the Institute ; and that of Mrs. Frederic Graff (1894–5), who has given the library a considerable collection of drawings and engravings of much historical interest, as a memorial of her late husband, Frederic

Graff, for many years a manager and vice-president of the Institute, and a member of the Committee on Library.

At the present time, the funds annually available for the purchase of new books, consist of the income derived from the "Bloomfield H. Moore Fund" and from the "Memorial Library Fund," amounting together to about $800, which is expended by the Committee on Library.

To provide a fund for binding and to meet current incidental expenses, the Board of Managers makes an annual appropriation from the general fund, which varies in amount according to the state of the finances, but which will average about $1,000.

It thus appears, that, taking no consideration of the additions made by deposits and gifts from official and private sources, the growth of the library is dependent upon the income derived from the several endowment funds (and which amounts to less than a thousand dollars annually), and upon the exchanges of the Journal. Without the invaluable aid derived from the last-named source, it is manifest that the provision for the library would be lamentably insufficient to meet even a fraction of its annual needs. Even with the aid of this powerful lever, the resources at the committee's disposal are inadequate to keep the library supplied with what is absolutely needful to keep it abreast of the progress of the arts and manufactures. *Funds available for buying books.*

What the committee needs for this purpose is an endowment fund of not less than $100,000, and, it is earnestly hoped that one of the first things accomplished when the Institute has realized its long-cherished plan for a new building, will be the making of such an adequate provision for the maintenance and growth of this important branch of its work. But, notwithstanding the fact that the committee's resources have always been greatly restricted, the library, thanks to the great benefits which it has continued to receive through the Journal, has suffered less from the ills of chronic poverty with which the Institute is afflicted, than some other *More liberal endowment needed.*

departments. At the present time (December 31, 1894), it numbers 41,812 bound and unbound volumes, 27,931 pamphlets (of which the greater portion is classified and catalogued), and 4,722 maps, charts, photographs, etc.

The library free for reference.

The entire library is *free* to the public, for reference, between the hours of 10 A. M and 3 P. M.

The library has never had the benefit of an adequate force of competent assistants, with the aid of whom much good work might be accomplished, not only in adding materially to the number of publications obtainable by gift, but also in proper classification and cataloguing. It may surprise those who are familiar with the working methods and needs of the modern library, to learn that all the domestic work of the Institute library—which is receiving monthly about 200 new volumes, issuing for reference 6,000 volumes monthly, and which has 150 readers per day—is performed by a single librarian, with the aid of one boy who also acts as messenger. This unfortunate state of things, which is due simply to the lack of funds at the Committee's disposal, greatly restricts the usefulness of the library, and imposes needless drudgery upon an officer whose time should be more profitably employed.

Overcrowded and in danger from fire.

In concluding this account of the library, it is proper that attention be called also to its greatly overcrowded condition, which seriously interferes with the duties of its custodians and the convenience of those who use it ; and, more serious by far, to the ever-present danger of destruction by fire, to which it is exposed in the present inadequately protected building in which it is housed. The destruction of the library, or of a large part of it, would be a loss well-nigh irreparable, and the fear of a calamity so grave should greatly stimulate the efforts of those members who are urging the project for a new building.

The Committee on Science and the Arts.

A branch of the Institute's work, which, perhaps, more obviously than any other, illustrates the utilitarian spirit which animated the founders, and which their successors have worthily perpetuated and striven to improve and extend, is that which is now conducted by the Committee on Science and the Arts.

One of the things that was, apparently, uppermost in the thoughts of the founders, was the need—as urgent then as to-day—felt by inventors and discoverers, of some competent, trustworthy and impartial body, to whom they could safely appeal for advice, and on whose judgment they could confidently rely for an opinion, as to the usefulness of their inventions and discoveries. *A committee to examine and report on inventions.*

One of the first acts of the Board of Managers was to make provision for this need. Article VIII of the original by-laws of the board, adopted at the stated meeting held February 26, 1824, made provision for the examination of "new machines or inventions which may be offered," and defined the mode of appointing committees for this purpose A year and a half later, this feature was permanently engrafted upon the parent body, by the repeal of this article, and the adoption of a substitute providing for a standing committee, to consist of five members, to be denominated the "Board of Examiners, whose duty it shall be * * * to examine and make report upon all new and useful machines, inventions and discoveries submitted to them." Subsequently the name of the Board of Examiners was changed to the "Committee on Inventions." *Organized in 1824.*

In his interesting address, delivered at the celebration of the fiftieth anniversary of the Institute, Mr. Fraley pays the following tribute to the activity and usefulness of this body:—

Early activity of the Committee on Inventions.

"The Committee on Inventions soon became a centre from which radiated the most useful and interesting results. The late Isaiah Lukens, a distinguished mechanician, was for many years its chairman, and, with the professors of the Institute, and such associates as Alexander Dallas Bache, Benjamin Reeves, Samuel V. Merrick, Rufus Tyler, Matthias W. Baldwin, John Agnew, George Washington Smith, John Wiegand and others, gave wise counsel to inventors, put them in the way of knowing what had previously been accomplished, saved them from the loss of money and of reputation by showing them when their inventions were not new, and, when any matter of real novelty or value was presented, endorsing it most heartily with their approval, and giving that potential aid which would almost certainly secure public recognition and reward."

This organization continued in existence until the year 1834, when, by act of the Institute, it was abolished, and in **Succeeded by the Committee on Science and the Arts.** its place there was established the "Committee on Science and the Arts," with enlarged powers and a wider field of labor. As originally constituted, membership in this committee was open to all members of the Institute in good standing who chose to enroll their names, and who, by thus voluntarily associating themselves with the committee, pledged themselves to perform the duties assigned to them. These duties were thus defined: * * * "to examine * * * all inventions that may be submitted, and to make detailed, descriptive reports thereon, giving their opinion with candor and impartiality on the inventions submitted, in the manner now practiced by the Committee on Inventions; * * * to conduct * * * such scientific investigations as may be deemed worthy of consideration, and to publish the results in the Journal of the Institute; * * * to inquire into and report upon the state of the arts generally, or into the state of any branch thereof, when called upon to do so, in order to disseminate useful practical information, or historical facts, in relation thereto; and * * * in general, (to assume) the scientific duties which devolve upon the institution, tending to mutual instruction, and to the dissemination of knowledge, and which are not specially entrusted by the constitution to the officers of the Institute."

Under this form of organization the committee continued for more than fifty years, and its usefulness during this long period is attested by its records, containing the results of the examination of a great number of inventions, and of its investigations of many subjects of importance entrusted to it by the Institute. The Journal, which it has enriched by the fruits of its labors, also bears eloquent testimony to their value, and to the industry and self-sacrifice of the long line of worthies whose names appear on its roll of membership. For many years its destinies were presided over by Alexander Dallas Bache, the great-grandson of Franklin, and whose profound and varied attainments in science, and eminent executive ability, were not unworthy of such distinguished ancestry. He was succeeded in the office of chairman by John C. Cresson, who, for many years, fulfilled the duties of the position with zeal and ability. *Usefulness of the committee.*

In the year 1886, the Institute adopted an amendment to its by-laws, by which this committee was reorganized on an elective basis, thus abolishing the plan of voluntary association which had heretofore been a distinguishing feature. By this amendment the Institute established a Committee on Science and the Arts, to be composed of forty-five members of the Institute, to be chosen at the annual election (fifteen each year), and "who shall pledge themselves by their acceptance of membership to perform such duties as may devolve upon them, and to sustain by their labors the scientific character of the Institute." *The committee made an elective body in 1887.*

Under this form of organization the committee exists at the present time, having substantially the same scope as its immediate predecessor, though, as will presently appear, endowed with somewhat enlarged powers. Thus, the Institute has confided to the committee the duty of awarding the

Its powers en-
larged.

gold medal endowed by the bequest of the late Elliott
Cresson, and to be awarded as a mark of recognition for
inventions and discoveries of pre-eminent value. The committee is likewise empowered to grant the silver " Medal of
Merit " founded by the bequest of our honored member and
ex-vice-president, Edward Longstreth, and a " Certificate
of Merit," and " Diploma," in cases which, in its judgment,
are deserving of such recognition.

A substantial proof of the value of this committee's
work, and which should be highly gratifying to every member
of the Institute, is afforded by the action of the Board of
Directors of City Trusts in availing itself of the committee's
services in the distribution of the " John Scott Legacy Medal
and Premium," to ingenious men and women who make
useful inventions. The committee has so carefully guarded
its recommendations of this award, which bears on the obverse
of the medal the inscription, "Awarded by the City of Philadelphia," that, thus far, in not a single case, has the Board of
City Trusts, to whose hands the city has confided the administration of the trust, failed to approve its judgments.

In the performance of its duties, the committee has ever
been seriously mindful of its responsibility to safeguard the
honorable reputation of the Institute, and has ever been actu-
ated by the desire to aid and encourage those who apply to
it for counsel and judgment. That its counsel should occasionally be distasteful, and its judgment the cause of disap-
pointment, and that it should occasionally have erred in both,
may be assumed as a matter of course, but the really
surprising thing about the committee, is the fact that in a
history covering nearly three-quarters of a century, it should
have made so few mistakes; and to its lasting credit should
be placed another fact, that the tongue of scandal has never
uttered a word in derogation of its honesty of purpose.

Since its organization in 1824, this body, besides making numerous investigations of special subjects referred to it
by the Institute, has examined nearly 2,000 inventions and

discoveries. To its counsel and aid, many worthy persons are indebted for the successful introduction of their inventions, and many others are indebted no less for having been dissuaded from wasting time and money upon worthless inventions and impracticable projects.

Since its reorganization on an elective basis, in 1886, not only has its work increased, but, having profited by the experience of the past, its methods, also, have been systematized and thereby improved, and in consequence, the standard of its reports has been raised. Membership in the committee is now regarded as a mark of distinction, which the ablest and most active members of the Institute are proud to gain. The sphere of its labors has expanded, and inventors and discoverers of other lands, attracted by the fame of its impartiality and the thoroughness of its reports, and seeking the honor of its approbation and rewards, not infrequently ask for its verdict on the merits of their productions.

It is fitting, in concluding this reference to the honorable career of an organization that has done so much to sustain the scientific reputation, and to increase the usefulness, of the Institute, to add the statement that the services of its members are rendered without compensation. When it is remembered that some of them are men of eminent attainments, and of the highest professional repute, and that all of them have been chosen by the Institute because of their special competency as experts in their respective trades or professions, the significance of this statement will be appreciated at its true value. It is no exaggeration to claim that there exists nowhere—either at home or abroad—in connection with any public institution of kindred character, an organization more directly useful in its aims, and more actively helpful in its work, than this committee; whose history should entitle it to a higher place in the esteem of good men and women; or whose mission would have been nearer to the heart of the great utilitarian and philanthropist with whose name, happily, it is associated.

The Journal.

The publication of a journal for the diffusion of knowledge on all subjects connected with the useful arts, was embraced in the plan of the founders, and was undertaken shortly after the organization had been effected. This publication has been continued without interruption to the present time, and has proved most useful, not only in directly promoting the aims and objects of the Institute, but also in extending the sphere of its influence beyond the limits of its local habitation.

The first step to secure a publication was taken by the Institute as early as 1825, when, by arrangement with C. S. Williams, publisher, a magazine bearing the title *The American Mechanics' Magazine*, and which had been founded by him in New York at the beginning of that year, was acquired by Dr. Thomas P. Jones, who had recently been elected professor of mechanics in the Franklin Institute. At the outset the responsibility of this venture appears to have been assumed by Dr. Jones, after he had received assurances of active co-operation and support from the members of the Institute, who were warmly interested in its success.

The prospectus of the new publication, which was issued August 1, 1825, announced the fact that "shortly will be published

THE
FRANKLIN JOURNAL
AND
MECHANICS' MAGAZINE,
UNDER THE PATRONAGE
OF THE
Franklin Institute, of the State of Pennsylvania, for the Promotion of the Mechanic Arts.
Edited by Doctor Thomas P. Jones, Professor of Mechanics in the Institute."

The object of *The Franklin Journal*, as defined in the prospectus, was, "to diffuse information on every subject connected with useful arts. In view of their subsequent Prospectus of the Franklin Journal. literal verification, the views of the editor, as set forth in his announcement, are worthy of reproduction here, especially since it is to his connection with the history of the enterprise, extending over a period of twenty-two years, that the Journal owes, in great measure, the attainment of that respected position at home and abroad as a reliable and useful exponent of the progress of American arts and manufactures, which it has been the constant aim of his successors worthily to maintain.

" In the accomplishment of this design," to quote from the prospectus, " the editor will freely avail himself of whatever has been published elsewhere; but he is determined, at the same time, to give to the work a character truly American. With this view, a particular description will be given of the various useful inventions and improvements made in our own country; and in selecting articles from foreign works, those of course will be preferred which are more immediately applicable to the arts and manufactures of the United States. A list of patented inventions will be given, accompanied with free remarks upon their utility and originality. Inventions either new, or not generally known, will occupy a large portion of the work. It will also contain brief reviews of works, whether foreign or domestic, which treat on any of the useful arts; descriptions of the productions of mechanical genius, remarkable either for their magnitude or for the skill and patience manifested in their execution; biographical notices of individuals who have distinguished themselves by the improvement or pursuit of the useful arts; exemplifications of the intimate connection which exists between science and skill in the mechanic arts, and of their dependence upon each other for the attainment of the utmost perfection of either.

" The transactions of the Franklin Institute and an abstract of the lectures delivered will always receive a distinguished place in its pages. * * *

"In the execution of this plan the Editor will not stand alone; he will be aided by his colleagues in the Institute, and by a number of other gentlemen distinguished by their zeal and capacity. His own resources are not inconsiderable as he has through life devoted a long portion of time to the attainment of knowledge in the theory and practice of the useful arts; has associated freely with mechanics and possesses sufficient skill to subject to the test of experience most of the processes which require an acquaintance with operative mechanics or chemistry; he pledges himself, therefore, never to mislead his readers on these subjects.

"The Editor will not be sparing of either time or money to render the work as perfect as possible. He is more anxious to make it useful than profitable, and is aware that if the latter quality is attained it must be through the medium of the former."

First issued in 1826.

The initial impression of the Franklin Journal was issued in January, 1826, and at the annual meeting of the Institute held January 19, 1826, it was "*Resolved*, That the members view with pleasure the prospect of the Franklin Journal being issued by so able an editor as the Professor of Mechanics in the Institute, and recommend it to the support of their fellow-citizens." In the report of the same meeting, it is stated that "Dr. Jones has undertaken the publication of the Journal on his own account, with the assistance of the members and under the patronage of the Institute."

Under this arrangement, and with certain aid from the treasury of the Institute, the Franklin Journal continued its career as a monthly magazine, until the close of the year 1827, when the Institute assumed the sole responsibility of its continuance. With the impression of January, 1828, it appeared as the Journal of the Franklin Institute, and thus has continued to the present.

The value placed by the Institute upon the services of Dr. Jones is evidenced by the fact that he was continued in the position of editor, and by the action taken at the quarterly meeting in April, 1828, at which it was announced that he Eminent ser-
vices of Dr.
Jones. would be compelled to sever his relations with the Institute, as professor of mechanics, in view of his acceptance of the office of Superintendent of the Patent Office, to which he had been appointed, April 12, 1828, and which required his removal to Washington. At the meeting above named, the Institute testified its appreciation of Dr. Jones' services in a resolution appointing him editor of the Journal during his life.

Dr. Jones continued his active relations with the Journal as editor until his death in 1848; and in the minutes of the meeting of the Institute held April 20, 1848, there appears a series of resolutions, passed on the announcement of his death, from which the following is condensed, to wit:—

Resolved, That the services of Dr. Jones, as the founder and able editor of the Journal of the Institute, from the time the publication of it was commenced until his death, * * * will ever be gratefully remembered by all who have participated in the labors and advantages of our Society.

In the prospectus of the Franklin Journal, above quoted, attention is called to the fact that it was intended to give a list of patented inventions, with remarks upon their utility and originality. This proposition was literally maintained and continued as a prominent feature of the Journal to the close of 1859, save that the " Remarks," which were in many cases of the greatest value to those interested in the progress of the arts and manufactures, were discontinued on the death of Dr. Jones. His accession to the position of Superintendent of the Patent Office naturally caused him to devote special attention to the preservation of the record of patents in the pages of the Journal. This circumstance has since proved of considerable value to all who have need to refer to the early patents of the United States, as will appear from the following explanation:—

In the official Patent Office publications, issued by the government prior to the year 1843, the publication of the

Valuable patent record. claims was omitted ; while, for a considerable period (1826–
1859), the Journal published an abstract of the specifications
and the claims in full, except for the patents of the years
1826 and 1827, and for those issued between the months of
March and October, 1836, during which intervals the publication of the claims, for some unexplained reason, was
omitted. The Journal, consequently, is the only source at
present available for reference to the specifications and
claims of patents issued by the United States, from 1828 to
1842, both inclusive, with the trifling omission of the eight
months of the year 1836, above noted. The Journal can also
be used, in place of the official publications, as a source of
reference to the patents granted during the entire period
(1826–1859) in which the patent lists were published therein.

Editors. Since the death of its founder, after twenty-two years of
service as its editor, the Journal has been conducted succes-
sively under the editorial management of Prof. Alexander
Dallas Bache, Mr. Chas. B. Trego, Prof. John F. Frazer, Dr.
Henry Morton, Dr. Wm. H. Wahl, Prof. George F. Barker,
and Mr. Robert Briggs.

From the year 1878, and down to the present, its super-
vision has remained in the hands of the Committee on Publications, under whose direct management the publication is
conducted with the editorial assistance of the Secretary of
the Institute.

Of late years, the abandonment of the plan of elementary
instruction, and the substitution of lecture courses having in
view the presentation of the latest advances in the useful arts,
and the expansion of the work of sections in the Institute,
have increased so considerably the amount of new and valuable material emanating directly from the scientific activity
of the Institute, as to have wrought a decided change in the
character of the Journal. While, formerly, the publication was, to a considerable extent, eclectic in make-up, it has
for a number of years been devoted, almost to the exclusion
of foreign matter, to the exposition of the actual work of the

39

Institute; the papers read at its meetings and before its sections, the lectures, and the work of its committees, affording an ample supply of material, much of it of the highest order of excellence.

In establishing the Journal, at the outset of the career of their organization, the founders "builded better than they knew." It has proved an invaluable aid in promoting the objects of the Institute. It has served the useful purpose of disseminating the results of the Institute's work, and thus of gaining for it a reputation at home and abroad, which no other instrumentality could have accomplished so effectively. It has placed the Institute on terms of active fellowship with the leading scientific and technical societies of America and Europe, by which it has been enabled to enrich its library with many thousands of volumes received in the form of exchanges. To-day it is one of the oldest publications in America devoted to science and the useful arts, and its pages, in addition to being the record of the useful work of the Institute, contain so many valuable contributions relating to the arts and manufactures in the United States, and to the progress of science and the arts in general, during the nearly three-quarters of a century of its existence, that it has come to be regarded, at home and abroad, as an indispensable work of reference.

The complete file of the Journal embraces the Franklin Journal, 4 volumes, 1826–1827; the Journal of the Franklin Institute (second series), 26 volumes, 1828–1840; the Journal of the Franklin Institute (third series), 109 volumes, 1841 to the present; or, 139 volumes in all. Since the publication of the general index, in 1890, the "series" designation of the Journal has been abandoned, the whole number being used to indicate the volume.

In its present form, the Journal is an octavo of 80 pages. It is published monthly, the twelve impressions being divided into two yearly volumes—January to June and July to December, each separately paged, and issued with title-page and index.

Its value in promoting the work of the Institute.

Exhibitions.

As a means of promoting the mechanic arts, the holding of exhibitions was highly favored by the promoters, and in this field of activity the Institute, for many years, was conspicuously prominent. It will be of interest here to reproduce, from the first quarterly report made to the Institute by the managers, in April, 1824, the language used in alluding to the project of holding an exhibition of American manufactures. This exhibition, it should be remembered to the credit of the Institute, was the first of the kind to be undertaken in this country. It was held in the month of October, 1824, in the old Carpenters' Hall, and, considering that at the time it was held, the Institute had been organized but a few months, the circumstances speaks eloquently for the energy and enthusiasm of the undertakers. The quarterly report above mentioned refers to this topic in the following words :—

"An object of equal, if not greater importance * * * is that of public exhibitions to which all the products of national industry may be sent; the effect and consequence of such exhibitions will necessarily be to extend the reputation of the Institute, to stimulate the zeal of the members, and to excite a proper degree of emulation and of justifiable rivalry among the numberless manufacturers and mechanics of this city. It is confidently believed that when the products of our industry are collected from the various workshops now dispersed throughout the city and State and exhibited together, they will form a collection calculated to excite a gratifying sense of pride in the bosom of every well-wisher to the prosperity of our manufacturers, and an encouraging hope that, under proper regulations, we may soon compete with foreigners in the manufacture of all useful articles."

The records which have been preserved of this first ex-hibition, demonstrate that it was looked upon as an event of the first importance. With the view of stimulating the ambition of the enterprising and of encouraging the domestication of new industries, special premiums were offered in advance for exhibits of new products and for such as should show notable improvement in quality.

One eye-witness of, and participant in, this historic event, happily, yet survives, linking with the span of more than ninety years, the present with the past—our revered Fraley. In his eloquent address on the occasion of the commemoration of the fiftieth anniversary of the Institute, which is replete with interesting and unique reminiscences, is the following reference to this event: "It was held in Carpenters' Hall in the autumn of 1824, and was crowned with complete suc-cess. It attracted large crowds of people who hitherto had had no conception of the extent and variety of our home productions, and reacted in many curious and unexpected ways to bring producers and consumers together, and to diffuse a knowledge of our domestic skill and resources."

Influence of the early Exhibitions.

The success which crowned their pioneer enterprise, gave such encouragement to our managers of early days, that it was followed, at brief intervals, by other exhibitions, during many years. The records of these exhibitions disclose many interesting facts relative to the origin and growth of the manufacturing arts in the United States; and the lists of premiums offered, afford the historians of our industries the materials for instituting instructive comparisons.

The solicitude displayed by the managers of these early exhibitions, to gain the confidence of exhibitors by fair treatment and by the conscientious devotion of time and skill to the examination of the merits of the exhibits, is strikingly shown in the published reports of these events, which are among the most highly valued of the Institute's records; and the conviction has often forced itself upon the writer, in reflecting on the subject, that the earnestness of purpose and devotedness, with which these men of the past generation labored to make the Franklin Institute useful and honored, have left an indelible impress upon the minds of those who have come after them, imbuing them deeply with the sentiment that loyalty to the Institute and jealous regard for its honor, are duties which have become theirs to maintain by right of inheritance.

Held yearly or biennially for many years. The exhibitions of the Institute were held yearly or biennially, down to the year 1858. They were held in various places. Many of the earlier events took place in the old Masonic Hall, on Chestnut street, above Seventh, and in a temporary annex thereto; and the more recent ones in the one-time famous Museum Building, at Ninth and Sansom streets, the destruction of which by fire, in the year 1850, made it necessary for the managers, for several years, to adapt themselves to less desirable quarters, and finally, to discontinue the exhibitions for a time, for want of a centrally located building suitable for the purpose.

The great value of these early exhibitions, down to the period above mentioned, was universally recognized throughout the country, and the reports and medals granted by the judges appointed to pass upon the merits of the exhibits were held in high esteem. The premiums and rewards offered to stimulate the ambition of the ingenious and enterprising, exerted the most beneficial influence in those days, when most of the manufacturing arts now flourishing famously in our midst were still in their infancy, or were yet unborn. They contributed, in no small degree, to the fruitful domestication on American soil, of new industries, to the substantial improvement of others already established, and to the development of the natural resources of the country.

The historian seeking for traces of the origin, and for evidences of the progress, of the industrial arts in the United States, finds in the records of the early exhibitions of the Franklin Institute a valuable fund of information; and, from this storehouse of facts—unimpeached and unimpeachable—

many treasures have been brought to light wherewith to enrich the pages of contemporaneous history. One writer on the history of the piano-forte dedicates his work, which is a valuable monograph on the subject, "To the Franklin Institute of Pennsylvania, which has exerted such a potent influence upon the early history of the American piano-forte and the kindred arts." Another, the author of a capital history of American pottery, is indebted for many important data to the information afforded by the records of these exhibitions, and to the *reliquiæ* preserved in the museum. No less appreciative of this valuable source of historic facts, is the author of the " History of Iron in All Ages ;" and the list could be lengthened were it needful to do so. In brief, so pronounced has been the influence of the early exhibitions upon the growth of our domestic industries, that, as one eminent writer on the subject concisely states the case, " No history of manufactures in the United States would be complete without reference to the work of the Franklin Institute." Records valuable to the historian.

In the year 1874 occurred the fiftieth anniversary of the Franklin Institute, and a fortunate circumstance enabled the managers to signalize the event by holding an exhibition, which proved from every point of view an eminently successful one. The circumstance spoken of was the fact that the Pennsylvania Railroad Co. placed at the service of the Institute, for exhibition purposes, the old building at Thirteenth and Market streets, for many years occupied as a freight station. The time, also, was propitious. Sixteen years had passed since an exhibition of the kind had been held in Philadelphia, and references to the Franklin Institute exhibitions had begun to savor of old-time reminiscences. Also, the near approach of the Centennial Exhibition had thoroughly aroused the interest of all classes of our citizens, who very properly considered the undertaking of the Institute in the light of a preparation for the great event to follow two years later. And, finally, the Institute was fortunate in having the services of an enthusiastic and industrious Committee on The Exhibition of 1874.

Exhibitions, under the leadership of a chairman admirably qualified for the position, and who devoted himself wholly, for the time, to the task of carrying the enterprise to a successful termination.

The principal facts relating to this brilliant exhibition are worthy of introduction in this place.

The address of President Coleman Sellers, on the occasion of the closing ceremonies, was particularly happy in its historic allusions, and in its references to the evidences, afforded by the exhibition, of the substantial advances that had been made in the character and quality of the exhibits, and especially to the evidences of the growth of a purer taste in design and decoration.

Some brief extracts from his remarks may appropriately be interpolated, viz.:—

Closing address of the President.

"I would gladly trace the progress in the arts during the past fifty years, could it be done in the limited time I dare address you; but I would be derelict in my duty, were I to fail to do so in one particular instance—because, it seems to me, great principles are involved. The machine display in this room is unquestionably very fine, and when one glances over that broad expanse of iron servants of man's will, and peers through the forest of belts that give motion to these machines, one cannot but be struck by the remarkable uniformity in color there shown, and doubtless may think the dark gray tint, the absence of all gay colors, indicative of our quaker tastes and habits. Ladies and gentlemen, there is to the student of a nation's art progress, more in that quiet color than can be traced to any such reason. The lesson it teaches is worth learning. Pardon me, if I repeat to you, the oft-told tale, of how man, in the helpless infancy of the race, with his naked hands alone, given him for defense or offense, fought his way in the great struggle for life, with clubs and stones as his only weapons. Clubs and stones were his only implements in tilling the land and ministering to his wants; but at all times did he try to beautify his tools or weapons, and a savage taste guided him in his selection of modes of ornamentation. Century upon century, as the people grew, so did their hands, aided by their growing minds, give them better, more efficient implements; and century by century these aids to man have grown into what we now see before us. These dumb servitors of mankind, with their frames of iron and their sinews of steel, which for life and motion devour the hard rocks of our anthracite, and in living and moving, breathe from their metallic lungs the hot vapors of steam, are doing our work better, ministering to our wants more freely than could thousands upon thousands of slaves.

"From the stone implements of the savage to what we now consider the highest type of mechanical skill, the desire to ornament, to beautify, has always guided the makers or their users. When machine-making became a trade, man, still seeking to satisfy his innate longing for the beautiful, borrowed from other arts, regardless of fitness, forms and colors of acknowledged beauty. He called to his aid every type of architecture, and decked his Gothic or Corinthian steam engine with all the gorgeous hues a painter's palette could offer him. As man's taste develops by culture he learns that beauty cannot be separated from fitness; that the most graceful forms, the most lovely colors fail to satisfy the eye when transported from their proper sphere or inharmoniously blended. It is an uneducated taste that finds satisfaction in brilliant colors only, or seeks to beautify uncouth forms by gorgeous paints ; while a higher culture fashions forms to suit the purpose for which they are designed, and colors them in subordination to their uses and surroundings. The grotesque architectural machinery of not many years ago is now seldom seen ; conventional forms, beautiful enough for some purposes when wrought in wood or stone, have been abandoned, so that, now, looking over this typical collection of machines for so many varied uses, we find that a new order of shapes, founded on the uses to which they are to be applied and the nature of the material of which they are made, have been adopted, and the flaunting colors, the gaudy stripes, and glittering gilding has been replaced by this one tint, the color of the iron upon which it is painted.

" That sombre tint is no indication of any quakerish objection to bright colors, but indicative of a higher culture and more refined taste. Two years hence, those who hear me now will perhaps think of this question of taste when they look at what other nations will send to our shores, and display, side by side with our work, yonder in our park. Americans, some years ago, had earned for themselves the reputation of a savage liking for gay colors in ornamentation, not common in other and older countries. That a great change has taken place in the right direction in machinery this wonderful exhibition testifies ; how far it has progressed in other trades I do not feel competent to judge, but I do feel very sure that the year 1876 will bring to us, in the greater exhibition—a nation will then hold—many a useful lesson in beauty in form, in humble objects ; in the art of surrounding ourselves and homes with forms of beauty that satisfy æsthetic tastes, and give color and grace to our living."

And the following allusion to the disposition, at that time, happily, more prevalent than now, to underrate the value of home productions, is worthy of a place in this sketch :—

"As president of a society that, for half a century, has labored zealously to promote the mechanic arts, I dare not lose this opportunity of saying a few words in the interest of American manufacturers. All observant visitors to this hall must have noticed goods displayed as of home make, which they had believed were always imported. Let me tell you, for I know it, there are prosperous industries in this city making goods of excellent quality, which you, ladies and gentlemen, purchase as of foreign make. The makers of these goods say they would find no purchasers should they mark them as Philadelphia made. Gentlemen, you select at your tailors', cloths that you are assured are the best imported goods. This may be so—in fact, really is in many cases—but the production of this country of looms to weave the finer cloths is a growing trade, and these looms send fine cloths into the markets, which, under fancy names, are sold. Ladies, I have held in my hand the wool—seen it carded on the finest machines, or combed for worsted yarns, * * * * * * spun into yarn and woven on American looms into the finest fabrics, you are now wearing—no, I would rather say that some other ladies are wearing, confident in the belief that they are decked in garments made in France, in England, in India—anywhere but in their own land. I will not say who is to blame for this, whether the manufacturer who hides his own name, the tradesman who buys the goods and sells them as imported, or we ourselves who think home-made articles not good enough for us. I would not have you purchase poor workmanship, because it is home-made, in preference to good work from abroad ; that will not compel progress in the arts ; but I would have you show a preference for what is well done in your own land.

Plea for home productions.

"Franklin, in memory of whose usefulness this Institute was named, discouraged the purchase of foreign finery, when our nation was so poor one hundred years ago. What he saw as a necessity in the light of self-protection then, may be less so now, for a wholesome tariff has shielded our workmen until home competition in well-organized business has enabled us to export what we used to import. The Franklin Institute, which was founded to promote the mechanic arts, asks your aid, your encouragement and preference for all the good work our mechanics can do."

The report of Mr. W. P. Tatham, the chairman of the committee, showed that, in addition to the members of the Institute, their ladies and children and others, who were admitted on free tickets, there were 267,638 paying visitors.

Summary of results.

"The number of applications for space was 1,528. The number of entries for exhibition, many of them covering numerous items and large displays, was 1,251. The number of steam boilers in operation was 9, of 316 horse-power in the aggregate, consuming 267 tons of coal. There were 3 steam engines driving shafting, 22 driving pumps, and 11 driving particular machines. The whole number of steam engines at work, or in motion, was 46. The whole number of machines in motion was 281.

"Some of the displays were of peculiar excellence. The photographs were particularly good, and would class strictly with the fine arts; but besides these, the variety and beauty of the chemicals displayed, the wonderworking of the sewing machines, the brilliancy of the saws, the splendor of the chandeliers, the rapidity of the printing press, the precision of movement of the machine tools, and the truth and finish of the paper cylinders, appealed not only to our appreciation of the usefulness of these exhibits, but in addition lent to them the charms and influences of the fine arts.

"As a further testimony to the excellence of the exhibition, it appears that although the rule on the subject of premiums, prepared by the proper committee and adopted by the Board of Managers, was more severe than usual, the premiums awarded under it were more numerous than at any previous exhibition; being 201 silver medals, 228 bronze medals and 222 certificates of honorable mention, in all 651, while many subjects were recommended to the Committee on Science and the Arts, for the award of the special medals of the Institute.

"* * * The results of our efforts prove the readiness of our people to visit a meritorious exhibition, and should encourage the managers of the great Centennial in hoping for a magnificent success to their undertaking."

The treasurer's account, finally, gave the further substantial proof of the conspicuous success of the exhibition of 1874, by showing a balance in favor of the Institute, after payment of all expenses, of $52,000.

An interesting item of history, which is referred to in the address of President Sellers, is the fact that the first definite proposition for the holding of an exhibition in commemoration of the Centennial Anniversary of the Independence of the American Colonies, originated in a memorial and resolution addressed to the Councils of the City of Philadelphia,

and which were adopted at the stated meeting of the Franklin
Institute in August, 1869.

Successful, however, as was the exhibition of 1874, it
was eclipsed in brilliancy, and in value from the educational
and technical standpoint, by that of 1884, which will ever   International
be memorable in the annals of the Franklin Institute. This   Electrical Ex-
was the Electrical Exhibition, held in the autumn of that   hibition, 1884.
year, under the direction of the Institute, and which by Act
of Congress, approved February 26, 1883, was made international in character. Of this exhibition, it has truly been
said, that, "measured by its results in stimulating the progress of electrical arts in the United States, it is acknowledged by all who are engaged in the electrical industries, to
have been by far the most important event of its kind ever
undertaken." It was the first exhibition in America devoted
exclusively to the electrical arts. Again, the time was
propitious. The electrical arts were just beginning to feel the
quickening impulse of that prodigious development which
has since fallen to their share, and which is the crowning
achievement of a century of wonderful scientific progress.
The public mind was in the condition of expectancy.
Dazzled by the brilliancy of a new-found light, that was to
banish darkness forever from our streets and homes, and by
other marvels in prospect, the public was ready to believe
anything, however extravagant, provided only that the magic
word, "Electricity" was uttered by way of explanation.

Again, the Institute was fortunate in securing, through
the friendly co-operation of the Pennsylvania Railroad Co.,
the use of the large station building at Thirty-second and
Market streets, in West Philadelphia, and of the adjoining
vacant lot owned by the company, bounded by Thirty-second
and Thirty-third streets, and Lancaster avenue and Foster
street, on which to erect an exhibition building especially
adapted for the purpose.

Again, the Institute was fortunate in having at its command the services of an able and enthusiastic committee of

its members, under the direction of a chairman of rare fitness for the post, possessed of executive ability of the highest order, and animated by an energy which his presence made contagious.

What it accomplished.
The result was successful beyond anticipation. It attracted the attention of the most eminent men of science in Europe and America, many of whom visited it and assumed the duties of judges; the reports of its experts in the various departments—but especially those in reference to the efficiency and life-duration of incandescent electric lamps, and on the efficiency of dynamo-electric machines—proved a contribution of permanent value to the scientific solution of these important problems; and its educational value as a great practical object-lesson to the pupils of the public schools of the city and vicinity—thousands of whom were admitted at a nominal charge, and for whom special facilities for studying the exhibition advantageously were provided in the form of elementary lectures and "primers" of electricity—can hardly be overestimated.

It is fitting to place on record here a few of the most important events of this great exhibition, gleaned principally from the report of Col. Chas. H. Banes, to whose conspicuous executive ability, as chairman of the Committee on Exhibitions, so much of the success of the enterprise is due, viz.:—

"In 1882 an electrical section of the Institute was established and the annual report of February, 1883, suggests the holding of a special exhibition devoted to electricity and its application to the arts.
"The suggestion was approved by the Institute and resulted in the decision to hold an International Electrical Exhibition. This was announced to open September 2, 1884, in a suitable building, built for its use, which occupied the block between Thirty-second and Thirty-third streets, on Lancaster avenue. The main structure was 283 feet in length by 160 feet in width, flanked by a tower 60 feet high at each corner. By a joint resolution of the United States Congress, articles from foreign countries designed for this exhibition were admitted free of duty.
"From the beginning of the work the exhibition committee had the cordial co-operation of the executive and the heads of departments of the government. These efforts were restricted, however, by the want of funds. Congress, while appropriating large sums of money to exhibitions at New Orleans and other cities, did not see fit to assist the Philadelphia exhibition except by resolutions. This failure rendered it necessary for the Franklin Institute to bear the expense incidental to the transportation and installing of government exhibits, and no money was spared to have the display made in a

creditable manner. The following departments were represented by interesting collections :— Governmentand historic exhibits.

"Ordnance Department, U. S. Army, in charge of Captain O. E. Michaelis.

"Ordnance Department, U. S. Navy, in charge of Lieutenant Bradley A. Fiske.

"U. S. Coast and Geodetic Survey, Treasury Department.

"Smithsonian Institution.

"U. S. Signal Office, in charge of Sergeant A. Eccard.

"These exhibits embraced instruments of precision as well as electrical apparatus. An attractive feature in the contributions of the U. S. Navy was a search-light of great power. This was mounted upon the northeast tower of the main building, and at night proved an object of great interest and wonder, as its powerful rays of light illumined distant parts of the city.

"In order that the progress of electrical science might be traced from its earliest history, by visitors and students, it was deemed advisable to prepare a special historical exhibit. In the rooms set apart for this purpose many valuable machines and models, loaned in response to requests of the committee, were arranged and attracted a great deal of attention. The historical report will present a list containing almost every invention of value in marking the development of electrical science. The most conspicuous in extent was the exhibit of the United States Patent Office. Over two hundred models, many of them of rare interest, were arranged on tables and so labeled as to clearly indicate their title and purpose. A complete list appears in the catalogue, and the committee appreciate the kindness of the Commissioner of Patents, and of Mr. C. J. Kintner, examiner in electricity, manifested in the loan and preparation of this display. Many individuals and firms added interest to the collection by sending machines of value. Prominent among the latter was the exhibition of Messrs. Wallace & Sons, Ansonia, Conn. This firm forwarded nine machines, among them the magneto-electric telemachon, for the development of power at a distance from its source. This was used at the Centennial in 1876. The Franklin Institute added to the interest of the collection by depositing some of its original Franklin apparatus.

"No portion of the vast collection in the electrical exhibition afforded greater interest for the thoughtful than the historical display. So great has been the progress in improvement since the House telegraph patent of 1846, the electric light patents of 1861, and the telephone patents of a still later date, that the famous first message of Prof. Morse has become a fitting legend for electrical progress, "What hath God wrought!"

In connection with this exhibition it should also be stated, that Congress in May, 1884, passed an Act, which was duly approved by the President, authorizing the appointment of a scientific commission,

"'which may, in the name of the United States government, conduct a national conference of electricians in Philadelphia in the autumn of 1884.' By virtue of this bill the 'United States Electrical Commission' was created for the purposes set forth. Professors Henry A. Rowland, George F. Barker, Simon Newcomb, C. F. Brackett, J. Willard Gibbs, John Trowbridge, F. C. Van Dyck, Charles A. Young, M. B. Snyder, E. J. Houston, Dr. Wm. H. Wahl, and Mr. R. A. Fisk, comprising the board, issued invitations to a large number of scientific gentlemen, both foreign and American, to assemble in conference. There was a large number of acceptances, and the meetings were held in September, first in the lecture hall of the exhibition and afterward at the building of the Franklin Institute. A perusal of the report of papers read and the discussions consequent thereon confirms the statement of the preamble to the bill creating the commission that 'The International National Conference of Electricians.

Electrical Exhibition offers a rare and fitting opportunity for such an official assemblage of electricians.'　　*　　*　　*　　*

"In addition to the schools, visiting in a body, a large number of other organizations, industrial and scientific, attended the exhibition during its progress. Among the latter were the United States Electrical Conference, the American Association for Advancement of Science, the British Association for the Advancement of Science, the Royal Society of Canada, the American Institute of Electrical Engineers, the American Institute of Mining Engineers, the New York Electrical Society, the Agassiz Association and others.

*　　*　　*　　"Among the foreign visitors to the exhibition were many scientific men of world-wide reputation. Prominent in the lists are recorded Sir Wm. Thomson, Lord Rayleigh, Prof. Sylvanus P. Thompson, W. H. Preece, Prof. George Forbes, Lieuts. F. R. DeWolski and Chrisholm Batten, official representatives of Great Britain; Prof. Tchisuke Fujoka, Tokio, Japan; F. N. Gisbourne, Government electrician for Canada; Señor Enriqua A. Mexia, official representative of Mexico; and others whose names appear among the members of the Electrical Conference."

With the view of utilizing to the utmost the unsurpassable educational facilities offered by this exhibition, a special committee was charged with the duty of arranging with the Board of Public Education of the city, and with the school authorities of neighboring cities and towns, to receive their pupils in a body at a reduced price of admission. The propositions of this committee were favorably received. The outcome is shown in the following extract from the chairman's report:—

An object lesson for the Schools.

"In response to a proposition made to the Board of Education of Philadelphia, the public schools of the city of the grades of high, normal, grammar, and unclassified, were granted each one day of vacation during the school term to attend the display. As the result of these arrangements, the official record of admissions shows an attendance, as organizations, of 97 schools, with 740 teachers and 16,657 students. In addition to these formal visits, there was an attendance at different periods of a number of sections and single classes.

"To facilitate the work of teachers in making the visits profitable to their pupils, arrangements were effected with professional men, familiar with electrical matters, to act as guides in explaining the uses of the machines, and the theories of electricity to the young visitors and without cost to them. This scheme proved of great value as a series of interesting object-lessons.

"A special inducement for study and observation of exhibits was offered the scholars of the public schools in the offer of prizes, consisting of a five-dollar gold piece, and an honorable certificate of the Franklin Institute for the best compositions on the subject, "What I saw at the Electrical Exhibition." The number of prizes distributed amounted to eighty, of which sixteen were secured by the High and Normal Schools, and the remainder by the Grammar and Unclassified Schools. In addition to these awards, two special prizes of ten and fifteen dollars were added by the *Electrical World*, of New York. These were distributed, with appropriate ceremonies, before a large audience assembled at the Normal School building, Thanksgiving night, November 27, 1884.　　*　　*　　*　　*

"To add still further to the educational attractions, arrangements were made for an excellent course of lectures, under the care of a committee appointed for the purpose. The report of the chairman is annexed, and will be found of interest, as illustrative of the high character of the lectures in their various specialties. For the public schools a special course upon electrical subjects was delivered by Prof. Houston. The school lectures were profusely illustrated, and, although necessarily elementary, were exceedingly interesting and profitable."

The work of the special "Committee on Bibliography," charged with the duty of preparing a collection of books and pamphlets relating to the subjects of electricity and magnetism, also proved highly successful, and the fruits of this labor, in the form of a valuable collection of electrical literature arranged in order, catalogued and dispayed in an apartment specially provided for it, added to the general interest of the exhibition. (The work of this committee is referred to more fully in the chapter devoted to the library.)

The direct practical results of this interesting undertaking are summarized in the following statement from the chairman's report :—

Results summarized.

"Total number of paid admissions was 282,779. The cash sales of tickets amounted to $98,639.70. * * *

"The report of the treasurer shows the exhibition to have been a financial success. The entire expense of erection of buildings, the cost of shafting, steam piping and general preparations, as well as the running expenses, were promptly met and a balance of a few thousand dollars left in the treasury. This was accomplished without government aid, or the use of public moneys."

In the year succeeding this memorable event the Institute held a "Novelties Exhibition," a general exhibition of the arts and manufactures, after the pattern of many that had preceded it. This was the twenty-ninth and latest exhibition held by the Institute.

The belief is very generally entertained, by those who have been active in past enterprises of this nature, that the great advances that have been made in the arts and manufactures in the United States, especially within the last two decades—in respect both of magnitude and diversification—have wrought so great a change in the relations sustained toward them by institutions like ours, that the day of general exhibitions under such patronage has gone by. The field to be covered is so vast, that to cover it adequately the resources of the State or the nation must be drawn upon. This is now the proper field of the great international displays. Much valuable work, however, may still be accomplished in the promotion of special branches of the arts and manufactures by the stimulating influence of exhibitions, and in this field of labor, it is hoped that the Institute which organized the first mechanics' exhibition ever held in the United States, will have many opportunities in the future of demonstrating to the world that it has lost nothing of its interest in the world's progress.

Special Investigations—
Reports and Public Work.

While much information of general interest, relating to Special Investigations. the activity of various departments of the Institute, has been relegated to the chapters specially treating of them, a large and important body of work, which has been accomplished by special committees, or otherwise, cannot conveniently be classified, and is accordingly presented in the following brief summary. This embraces a reference to the more prominent Public Work. only of the many good works of the Institute, not elsewhere referred to, and which are worthy of placing on record for the information of the curious, and for the guidance of the future historian. That this record is imperfect, and that it does scant justice to an institution that has, throughout its whole career, been unceasingly active in works of utility which do not obtrude themselves upon public notice, none is more conscious than the writer.

For many interesting facts bearing on the early activities of the Institute, the writer is indebted to the interesting historical address of the Hon. Frederick Fraley, delivered at the celebration of the fiftieth anniversary of the Institute in February, 1874. For those of the more recent period he speaks from personal knowledge. They are accordingly arranged in their chronological order, as the most natural and the most convenient mode of reference.

The first work of general public importance undertaken Report on water power. by the Institute, was the investigation of the various forms of water-wheels for giving economical value to water-power. "On this subject," to quote our venerable historian, "experiments in great number, and on almost every form of water-motor then known, were made, and the results tabulated and commented on in such an exhaustive manner that this report continues to this day to be a most valuable text-book on water-power.

"Following this, and in the same line of practical usefulness, a committee was formed to investigate the cause of the explosion of steam boilers; and in this investigation the committee succeeded in getting the co-operation of the government of the United States, an appropriation for defraying the cost of the experiments being made by Congress, but no part of the money so appropriated was paid as compensation to the experimenters. These were all volunteers, devoting many months of valuable time to the investigation, and ascertaining most valuable facts, which have since been utilized for the benefit and safety of the public."

Closely connected with these experiments, and naturally growing out of them as the investigation progressed, was an inquiry into the strength of materials used in construction. "For this purpose," our historian says, "the committee devised testing apparatus of various forms, and applied them in the most extensive and crucial way to the metals and materials of all kinds used in machines, steam boilers, buildings and other branches of the useful arts."

These investigations, the results of which were published *in extenso* in the Journal, formed a contribution of the utmost value to manufacturers of steam machinery, architects and builders. These publications were widely quoted abroad, and for many years were regarded as the most authoritative source of information on the subjects to which they relate.

At the instance of the government, the Institute made an elaborate investigation and report on the subject of the suitability of various building stones, with especial reference to the selection of the stone best adapted to be used in the construction of the Delaware Breakwater.

At the request of the Legislature of Pennsylvania, the Institute examined and reported on our system of weights and measures. Our historian records, that "a special committee was called" for this purpose, "which thoroughly went through the work, and upon its report, the law was enacted which is now in force for the commonwealth." **Weights and measures.**

The public interest awakened in the subject of meteorology by the lectures and essays of Prof. James P. Espy, and by the active discussion of the rival theories of storms, advanced and defended, respectively, by Espy and Redfield, caused the Institute, in the year 1843, to apply to the Legislature of Pennsylvania for a grant of money to be devoted to the purchase of instruments for the equipment of stations throughout the State for the systematic observation and collection of meteorological facts. This application was successful, and an appropriation of $4,000 was made for the purpose, the expenditure of which was left in the hands of the Institute. **First Weather Bureau, 1843.**

This circumstance seems to have special interest, inasmuch as it is the earliest instance on record, of which the writer is aware, of the appropriation, in any country, of public funds for the collection of facts relating to the weather.

With the aid of this appropriation, the Committee on Meteorology of the Institute, in conjunction with a similar committee appointed by the American Philosophical Society, purchased instruments of precision, organized a corps of observers, and for a number of years conducted a system of simultaneous meteorological observations for the intelligent study of weather phenomena. This work was gradually extended, and at length was carried on with the assistance of voluntary observers in all parts of the United States. The data were tabulated and published, together with the results derived from their study and discussion. For many years after this committee had abandoned the active prosecution of this work, the collection of weather data by some of these observers was continued, and the monthly summary of their observations was a conspicuous feature in the Journal.

One of the valuable results of this early meteorological work was the formulation of a theory of storms, which is substantially the same as that at present accepted as the correct one. This work, accomplished before the day of the telegraph, may be regarded as the first step towards the creation of the present highly elaborate system of weather

Present State Weather Service organized 1887. bureaus of this and other countries, and which have proved of such inestimable benefit to commerce and agriculture. In 1887, the Legislature of Pennsylvania, at the suggestion of the Franklin Institute, provided the means for the establishment of a State Weather Service for Pennsylvania, which was organized by the Institute, with the co-operation of the United States Weather Bureau, and is to-day in a creditable state of efficiency. Weather stations, equipped with apparatus, have now been established in almost every county of the State, and a highly-trained corps of volunteer observers is engaged in the collection of weather data. These data are duly tabulated and published, under the direction of the Committee on Meteorology of the Institute, in the form of monthly bulletins, weather maps, weekly crop bulletins, etc., and afford the material for a complete study of the climatology of the State.

Standard screw-thread. In 1864, the Franklin Institute made an inquiry into the subject of the shape and proportions of screw-threads used in machine construction. This inquiry was made by a special committee appointed for the purpose, and its report, which was adopted at the meeting of the Institute held in March, 1865, recommended for adoption by machine builders throughout the United States, a uniform and simplified system of screw-threads, which, within a few years thereafter, was officially adopted by the government, and, under the designation of the "United States or Franklin Institute Standard Thread," is now in universal use throughout the country.

The Associated Engineering Societies of Germany, after diligent inquiry into the merits of the systems in vogue in all countries reported, in 1887, in favor of the adoption, for the German Empire, of a system of threads having the distinctive form of the Franklin Institute thread, but adapted, as to proportions, to the requirements of the metric system.

In 1875, the Councils of the City of Philadelphia appropriated the sum of $1,000 for the expenses of an expert commission to be nominated by the Franklin Institute, and, with the approval of the Mayor, to act in conjunction with the Chief Engineer of the Water Department, to which commission was referred the subject of the present and the future water supply of Philadelphia. This boby performed its allotted task, and the results of its labors appear in an elaborate report to the Councils, of which an abstract was published in the Journal for November, 1875. *Water supply for Philadelphia.*

In another field the Institute also did valuable pioneer work; namely, in the investigation, by special committee, of the efficiency of the dynamo-electric machine for arc-lighting. This investigation, which appears to have been the earliest intelligent inquiry into the relative merits of the several types of these machines, was made in the year 1878, and the results of the committee's work appear in the Journal for May and June of that year. The report of this committee attracted at the time widespread attention, and was quoted, with many flattering comments, in the scientific publications of the world. *Dynamo-electric machines.*

In 1884, the Institute supplemented its earlier work in this field by a more elaborate report on the same subject, and on the "Life-Duration and Efficiency of Incandescent Electric Lamps," in connection with the International Electrical Exhibition, held under its patronage in that year, and to which an extended reference will be found elsewhere. Closely allied to these investigations is its report on "The Conditions of Safety in Electric Lighting," published in the Journal for December, 1881, and which formulated for the first time a number of the "conditions" to be observed in the wiring of buildings and the running of circuits, which *Incandescent lamps.*

have since become incorporated in the regulations of the Fire Underwriters' Associations.

It would easily be possible greatly to extend the preceding list, but, as stated at the outset of this section, it has been the writer's purpose to designate only the more prominent events in the long and honorable career of the Institute, and which could not conveniently be brought under other chapter heads.

Incomplete though this summary undoubtedly is, it will nevertheless suffice to give the reader, who may be interested in the history of the Franklin Institute, a fair impression of its continued activity in works of public utility.

APPENDIX.

ORGANIZATION.

Officers and Managers of the Franklin Institute.

President................Joseph M. Wilson.
First Vice-President .....Charles Bullock.
Second Vice-President....William P. Tatham.
Third Vice-President.....Henry R. Heyl.
Secretary................William H. Wahl.
Treasurer ....Samuel Sartain.

Auditors....W. O. Griggs, Samuel H. Needles, Francis Leclere.

Actuary,
H. L. Heyl.

Librarian,
Alfred Rigling.

Board of Managers,

Joseph M. Wilson, *ex off., Chairman.*

Chas. H. Banes,	Edward Longstreth, *ex off.,*
Arthur Beardsley,	M. R. Muckle, Jr.,
Henry Bower,	Isaac Norris, Jr.,
Charles Bullock, *ex off.,*	Lawrence T. Paul,
Thos. P. Conard,	Henry Pemberton, Jr.,
Chas. H. Cramp,	Horace Pettit,
George V. Cresson,	Theorore D. Rand,
Chas. G. Darrach,	Stacy Reeves,
F. Lynwood Garrison,	Sam'l P. Sadtler,
Alfred C. Harrison,	Samuel Sartain, *ex off.,*
Henry R. Heyl,	Coleman Sellers,
Edwin J. Houston,	William P. Tatham, *ex off.,*
H. W. Jayne,	William H. Thorne,
Washington Jones,	J. C. Trautwine, Jr.,

William H. Wahl, *ex off.*

Curators,

Stacy Reeves, Washington Jones.

Professors,

Coleman Sellers, E. D., Professor of Mechanics.
Edwin J. Houston, Ph. D., Professor of Physics.
Sam'l P. Sadtler, Ph. D., Professor of Chemistry.
F. Lynwood Garrison, Professor of Economic Geology,
Mining and Metallurgy.

Board of Trustees,

Joseph M. Wilson, President.

Enoch Lewis,	John T. Morris,
J. Vaughan Merrick,	William Sellers,

Samuel Sartain.

CHARTER AND BY-LAWS OF THE FRANKLIN INSTITUTE

OF THE STATE OF PENNSYLVANIA FOR THE PROMOTION OF THE MECHANIC ARTS.

An Act to amend and alter the Act incorporating the Franklin Institute of the State of Pennsylvania for the promotion of the Mechanic Arts.

Wheras: The Act approved March thirtieth, one thousand eight hundred and twenty-four, incorporating the Franklin Institute of the State of Pennsylvania, for the promotion of the Mechanic Arts, has been found insufficient and inconvenient for accomplishing the objects of said corporation, and the said corporation has applied for alteration and amendment thereof.

Section 1. *Be it enacted by the Senate and House of Representatives of the Commonwealth of Pennsylvania, in General Assembly met, and it is hereby enacted by the authority of the same,* That the present members of said corporation, and all such person as may hereafter become members thereof, shall be, and are hereby created a body politic and corporate by the name of the " Franklin Institute of the State of Pennsylvania for the Promotion of the Mechanic Arts," and shall have perpetual succession, be able to sue and be sued, to plead and be impleaded, to have and use a common seal, and the same to break, alter, and renew at pleasure, and shall be able to take, hold, purchase, and enjoy such real and other estates of any nature or kind whatsoever as they may obtain by purchase, devise, bequest or gift, and the same at their pleasure to sell, lease, mortgage, pledge, encumber, or dispose of as they may deem proper or convenient for promoting the objects of the said corporation ; and the said corporation shall have the like power over any real or other estates now owned or held by them ; *provided*, that the clear yearly value of the real estate at any time held by them shall not exceed ten thousand dollars.

Sect. 2. That it shall be lawful for the said corporation to raise funds for the payment of its present indebtedness, and for all other purposes of the said corporation, to create and sell such number of shares of stock, at ten dollars each, as may be deemed proper to represent the estates of the said corporation, and the certificates of such stock shall be in such form, be transferable in such manner, subject to such payments, and entitle the holder thereof to such privileges, as the said corporation may, by its by-laws in reference to such stock, grant and direct.

SECT. 3. The object of the said corporation shall be the promotion and encouragement of manufactures and the mechanical and useful arts, by the establishment of lectures on the sciences connected with them, by the formation of cabinets of models, minerals, machines, materials and products, by exhibitions and premiums, by a library and by all such measures as they may judge expedient.

SECT. 4. The members of the said corporation shall consist of manufacturers, mechanics, artisans, and persons friendly to the mechanic arts, and of such stockholders in said corporation as may, by the by-laws, be entitled to the privileges of members ; and every member shall pay such sum for an annual or life subscription as the by-laws of said corporation may require ; and honorary and corresponding members may be elected at such times, and in such a way, and with such privileges as said corporation may deem expedient.

SECT. 5. The said corporation shall be managed in such way, and by such number of officers, managers and other persons as the by-laws may prescribe ; and the powers and functions of such officers, managers and other persons, the rights and duties of members, the manner of their election, and the causes which may justify their expulsion or suspension, and all other concerns of the said corporation, shall be fixed and regulated by its by-laws, which by-laws shall be adopted by said corporation at the first monthly meeting after the acceptance of this amended Charter, and said by-laws shall be altered and amended only in the manner provided in said by-laws as then adopted.

SECT. 6. So much of the Act to which this is a supplement as is inconsistent herewith is repealed.

OFFICE OF THE SECRETARY OF THE COMMONWEALTH
OF PENNSYLVANIA, APRIL 25; 1864.

I certify that the foregoing bill passed both branches of the Legislature, and received the signature of the Governor on this day. As witness my hand the day and year above written.

(Signed)   ELI SLIFFER,
                                    Secretary of the Commonwealth.

BY-LAWS.

ARTICLE I.—*Trustees.*

SECTION 1. All Real and Personal Estate of the Institute which may hereafter be acquired by voluntary subscription or devise, bequest, donation, *or in any way other than through its own earnings or by investment of its own funds*, saving where the donors shall expressly provide to the contrary, shall be taken as acquired upon the condition that the same shall be vested in a Board of Trustees who shall be appointed in the manner hereinafter indicated. Unless the title to such property shall be directly vested in said Board of Trustees by the donors, the Institute, by deed attested by the President and Secretary, which they are hereby authorized to execute and deliver, shall forthwith convey the same to said Trustees, who shall hold it in trust for the purposes specifically designated by the donors; or, if there shall be no specific designation, for the benefit of the Institute in the way and manner hereinafter provided, so that the same shall not, in any event, be liable for the debts of the Institute.

SECT. 2. Said Board of Trustees shall be composed of seven (7) members, who shall be elected as follows:—

They shall be nominated at a stated meeting of the Board of Managers, at least one (1) month prior to the election. They shall be elected by a vote of two-thirds (⅔) of the members present.

In case of a vacancy occurring in the Board of Trustees, it shall be filled as follows:—

The Board of Trustees shall nominate to the Board of Managers three (3) suitable persons, and the Board of Managers shall elect one (1) of the three (3) to fill the vacancy.

The *remaining* members of the Board of Trustees, whenever at any time it shall be deemed necessary so to do, shall have power to assign and convey the property held by them, so as to vest the title thereto in themselves and their successors.

SECT. 3. Said Trustees shall have full power and authority, from time to time, to assign, sell and dispose of any property, real and personal, by them held, unless there shall be some direction by the donors to the contrary, and shall have power to convey the same without purchasers being obliged to see to the application of the purchase moneys, when authorized so to do by a vote of two-thirds (⅔) of the members present at any regular or special meeting of the Board of Managers, *provided*, that they shall not be obliged to sell or convey unless a majority of their own Board shall also approve.

SECT. 4. Said Trustees shall not be confined to legal investments, but shall have full power to invest in any real property, improvements and alterations, and in any securities, other than shares of stock, or unusual personal obligations, which to them may seem advisable. They shall take such care and control of the property as is usual and proper.

SECT. 5. Said Trustees shall have power to appoint agents to act for them, and for the acts of such agents they shall not be personally responsible where they have exercised ordinary prudence in selecting them.

SECT. 6. Said Trustees shall have power to carry into effect any special trusts upon which any property may be held by them. They shall pay out all necessary and proper costs, charges and expenses, and from time to time shall pay over the net income, unless otherwise directed by the donors, to the Board of Managers, to be applied by them, under the instructions of said Trustees, to the general uses of the Institute. The same, however, not to be liable to the debts thereof, but so that the continuance and efficiency of the Institute shall be preserved.

SECT. 7. At the annual meeting of the Board of Managers in each year, said Board of Trustees shall present a report of their proceedings and a detailed statement of their receipts and expenditures for the year. An approval of such account shall be final and conclusive, and shall bar any right to demand any other or further accounting.

SECT. 8. The Board of Trustees, at a meeting of the members of the Institute, called after three (3) months' special notice, at which the holders of nine-tenths ($\frac{9}{10}$) of the whole outstanding shares of stock shall vote affirmatively, may convey all property, real and personal, in them vested, to the Institute, free and clear of all trusts; *provided*, that there be no specific trusts violated by such conveyance, and that all the members of said Board, as the same shall then be constituted, shall approve of such conveyance.

ARTICLE II.—*Stock*.

SECTION 1. The Real and Personal Estates of the Institute as held upon the First Day of January, One Thousand Eight Hundred and Eighty-one, shall be valued at *One Hundred Thousand Dollars*, and shall be represented by *Ten Thousand Shares* of Stock of the par value of *Ten Dollars* each. Said shares shall be divided into two classes, viz. :—

First Class.—Shares not registered for use : on which no annual payment shall be charged or collected, and the holders thereof shall not have the privileges of members of the Institute, but may, if of legal age, vote at any annual election for officers, managers and auditors, upon the payment of *One Dollar* upon each share of stock on which they may desire to vote; *provided, however*, such shares have been held by the same person at least three months before such election.

Shares of the First Class may be converted into shares of the Second Class, at the pleasure of the owners, provided the transfer be approved by the Board of Managers; but, when once so converted, they shall always continue in the Second Class.

Second Class.—Shares registered for use : on which *Six Dollars* per annum shall be due and payable in advance on the first day of October in each year, except as hereinafter provided.

All subscriptions to stock shall be approved by the Board of Managers before the certificate can be issued.

SECT. 2. The holders of Second Class stock shall be entitled to the use of the library, lectures and reading-room ; and, if of legal age, to all other privileges of membership in the Institute, so long as they make the annual payment in advance; and shall, on the payment of *One Dollar* therefor, be entitled to a Certificate of Membership.

SECT. 3. If the annual dues for two successive years remain unpaid at the expiration of two and a half years on any share of stock of the Second Class, such share shall then become forfeited to the Institute ; but such forfeiture may be remitted by a unanimous vote of the Board of Managers.

SECT. 4. Certificates for the First Class stock may be issued for any number of shares in a single certificate ; but every certificate for the Second Class shall be for one share only.

SECT. 5. All certificates of stock shall be signed by the President and Secretary ; shall be issued by the Actuary, and shall be transferable only on the books of the Institute by the owner, or his legal representative, on the surrender of the old certificate, and on the payment of the Stamp Tax, and of a fee of *twenty-five cents* for each certificate.

SECT. 6. No share of stock in the Second Class shall be transferred until all arrearages and fines are paid, and all books and tickets returned, and the transfer approved by the Board of Managers.

SECT. 7. The shares of stock obtained by the Institute by legacies, donations or forfeiture, shall at once be canceled.

ARTICLE III.—*Members.*

SECTION 1. The members of the Institute shall consist of manufacturers, mechanics, artisans, and persons friendly to the mechanic arts, and they may be either annual contributors, life members, permanent members, holders of Second Class Stock, honorary or corresponding members.

SECT. 2. The name, occupation and place of business or residence of any persons, other than a holder of Second Class stock, desirous of becoming a member, shall be entered in a book (kept for the purpose in the Hall of the Institute, always open for inspection) by any member of the Institute, who shall enter his own name at the same time with that of the candidate whom he proposes. These names so proposed shall be acted upon by the Board of Managers from time to time.

SECT. 3. The privileges of membership in the Institute shall extend only to persons of legal age who are not in arrears and who shall have signed the charter and by-laws.

SECT. 4. Honorary and corresponding members shall be nominated by the Board of Managers, and shall require for their election four-fifths of the votes of the members present at any meeting at which their nomination may be acted upon.

SECT. 5. Members shall be entitled to a Certificate of Membership on payment of *One Dollar*.

SECT. 6. Resignations of membership shall be made to the Board of Managers in writing, but shall not be accepted until all dues, fines, and arrears of dues at the rate of seventy-five cents a month, subsequent to the first of October and up to the date of resignation, shall have been paid, and books and tickets returned.

SECT. 7. Members whose yearly dues are in arrears for more than three years shall be considered as having resigned, and the Actuary is directed to strike their names from the list of members.

ARTICLE IV.—*Payments.*

SECTION I. The annual dues of contributing members shall be eight dollars; a life membership (not transferable) may be acquired by the payment of one hundred dollars within any one year; and a permanent membership may be granted to any one who shall, within any one year, contribute to the Institute the sum of one thousand dollars, which membership may be transferred by will or otherwise.

SECT. 2. Holders of Second Class stock and contributing members enrolled as non-resident members shall pay upon election to membership an entrance fee of five dollars and an annual fee of two dollars.

SECT. 3. Stock of the Second Class may be held in trust for persons not of legal age, and shall be liable to the payment of only one-half the annual fees due upon stock of Second Class held by persons of legal age; *provided*, that when such minors arrive at legal age, new certificates, subject to the full annual contribution, shall issue on payment of the customary fee.

Sect. 4. The annual payment of fees for membership shall be due and payable on the 1st of October in each year, in advance; but all members elected after the 31st of January in each year shall pay, in advance, at the rate of *seventy-five cents* a month to the 1st of October next ensuing.

Sect. 5. The annual dues from contributing members may be applied to the current expenses of the Institute, but all moneys received from life and permanent membership shall be vested in the Board of Trustees, the income therefrom only to be applied to the maintenance fund.

Article V.—*Officers*.

The Officers shall be a President, three Vice-Presidents, a Secretary, a Treasurer, twenty-four Managers, and three Auditors. Two-thirds of the Managers shall be manufacturers or mechanics.

Article VI.—*Election of Officers*.

Section 1. An election for officers shall be held on the third Wednesday in January in each year. At this election the President, the Secretary and the Treasurer shall be elected to serve one year, and one Vice-President, eight Managers, and one Auditor shall be elected to serve for three years; *provided*, that the officers now elected, or who may hereafter be elected, shall continue to serve until their successors be elected. No person shall be allowed to vote unless all his arrears are paid.

Sect. 2. All elections for officers of the Institute shall be by ballot, and no vote shall be cast by proxy.

Sect. 3. The President shall, at the stated meeting in December, annually, appoint seven members of the Institute to conduct the election for officers to be held on the third Wednesday in January, and to act as judges of said election. They shall meet at the Hall of the Institute at 4 o'clock P. M. on the day of the election, then and there open the polls for said election, keeping the polls open until 8 o'clock P. M., and making a record of the name of each voter. On the closing of the polls they shall forthwith count the votes and report the result to the President.

In case any one or more judges of said election shall fail to attend, the judges present on the day of the election shall have power to fill the vacancies.

ARTICLE VII.—*President.*

It shall be the duty of the President, or, in his absence, of one of the Vice-Presidents, in order of seniority of election, or, in their absence, of a President to be chosen *pro tempore*, to preside at all meetings of the Institute and of the Board of Managers, preserve order therein, put all questions, and announce all decisions.

ARTICLE VIII.—*Secretary.*

SECTION 1. The Secretary of the Institute shall be a person of scientific and literary attainments, and shall receive such annual compensation for his services as may be fixed by the Board of Managers.

SECT. 2. His duties shall be to receive members and strangers visiting the Institute; to take charge of the library, cabinets, and other property of the Institute under the direction of the various Committees and Curators; to present and read at each meeting of the Institute a statement of such scientific discoveries, mechanical improvements, or novelties in the arts or engineering, as he may deem of interest to the members; and to perform such other duties as he may deem advisable to promote the objects of the Institute, or such as may from time to time be designated by the Institute. He shall also answer all letters addressed to the Institute except those relating to stock, finance, or of a business character; open and maintain such correspondence as may promote its interest; notify honorary and corresponding members of their election, and Committees of the Institute of their appointment, and acknowledge all donations to the library or cabinets in the *Journal*, and to the donors thereof at his discretion. He shall report, or cause to be reported, the proceedings of the Institute, and shall deliver the report thereof, or an abstract of it, to the editor for publication.

SECT. 3. In case of the absence or sickness of the Secretary, it shall be the duty of the President to appoint a person to perform the duties of the position *pro tempore.*

SECT. 4. A suitable person shall be appointed by the Secretary, with the sanction of the Board, to act as Librarian.

ARTICLE IX.—*Treasurer.*

It shall be the duty of the Treasurer to receive from the Board of Trustees all funds, which they may pay over to the Board of Managers in accordance with Section 6 of Article I. He shall also receive all moneys collected for the Institute by the Actuary. He shall deposit all moneys received, in the name of the corporation, in such institution as the Board of Managers may direct. He shall make no payments without written vouchers from the Board of Managers. He shall keep accurate accounts of the income and disbursements of the Institute, exhibit an accurate statement of his receipts and payments at each stated meeting of the Board of Managers, and of the condition of the finances of the Institute whenever called on by them, and shall make an annual statement thereof at the annual meeting of the Institute. He shall give bonds to an amount fixed by the Board of Managers for the faithful performance of his trust. In case of a vacancy in the office of Treasurer, it shall be the duty of the Board of Managers to appoint a person to perform the duties of the position *pro tempore*.

ARTICLE X.—*Auditors.*

The Auditors shall examine the Treasurer's accounts and compare them with the orders of the Board of Managers, and report to the Board as to their correctness. They shall also examine the accounts of the Trustees, and report the results to the Board of Managers.

ARTICLE XI.—*Organization and Government of Sections.*

SECTION 1. For the promotion and encouragement of manufactures and the mechanic arts, as well as of the sciences connected with them, members of the Franklin Institute may form sections and hold meetings in the Hall, or such other rooms as may be provided for them by the Board of Managers. These sections shall be constituted as hereinafter provided, and shall have precedence in the order of their formation.

SECT. 2. Any number of members, not less than twelve, may constitute a section.

SECT. 3. Members desiring to form a section shall make written application to that effect to the Committee on Sectional Arrangements, which committee shall report such applications, from time to time, to the Board of Managers at one of its stated meetings, with such recommendations as the Committee may deem it expedient to make in each case.

An application for the formation of a section shall be made in the following form :—

" The undersigned, members of the Franklin Institute, request that they may be constituted the ——— Section of the Franklin Institute."

This application, when submitted by the Committee on Sectional Arrangements, shall be considered by the Board of Managers, and, if approved by the Board, the section shall be established and the names of the petitioners shall be recorded on the minutes as the founders of that section, and shall be reported by the Board of Managers to the Institute at its next meeting. Whenever the petitioners have organized, they shall report such organization, with the names of their officers, to the Committee on Sectional Arrangements. But if they shall fail to organize such section within six months after the date of said approval, or if an established section shall fail to make a report of its proceedings to the Committee during any period of twelve months, it shall be the duty of the Committee on Sectional Arrangements to inform the Board of Managers, which may thereupon declare that such section is extinct.

SECT. 4. All members of the Institute shall have the privilege of enrolling themselves, without payment of additional fees, as members of any of the sections which are now, or which may hereafter be, established in conformity with these by-laws, and such enrollments shall be reported from month to month to the secretaries of the sections designated; but no person shall be entitled to any of the privileges of any of the sections who has not complied with the conditions of Section 3 of Article III of these by-laws.

SECT. 5. Each section shall submit to the Committee on Sectional Arrangements prior to the stated meeting of the Board of Managers in December of each year, an estimate of moneys it will require for the ensuing year, and such estimate the Committee on Sectional Arrangements shall transmit, with its recommendation, to the Board at its stated meeting in December.

SECT. 6. Each section shall elect its own officers and make its own by-laws, not inconsistent with the charter and by-laws of the Franklin Institute. The Institute shall not be responsible for bills contracted by any section except in conformity with the conditions prescribed in Section 4 of Article XII of the by-laws relating to committees, nor in any event for a sum greater in any one year than the amount appropriated by the Board of Managers for the service of the section for that year.

SECT. 7. All requisitions for supplies shall be made by order upon the Actuary of the Institute.

SECT. 8. The books, papers, apparatus, specimens, models, and all other collections of each section, shall be the property of the Institute, held for the use of that section. Donations of objects or books to or for any section, shall be received and reported to the Committee on Sectional Arrangements, and by this Committee to the Board of Managers, as donations to the Institute for the use of that section.

SECT. 9. At the first meeting of each section it shall determine, subject to the approval of the Board of Managers, the times of its stated meetings.

SECT. 10. Papers read and lectures delivered before any section and approved by the same, shall be referred to the Committee on Publications of the Institute, and, if accepted by them, shall be published in the *Journal* of the Institute.

SECT. 11. Societies now existing, or which may hereafter be founded, for the consideration of any subjects clearly within the scope of the Franklin Institute, and which societies may desire to unite with the Franklin Institute as sections, shall furnish a list of such of their members as have declared their willingness to become members of the Institute, to the Committee on Sectional Arrangements, which committee shall transmit the same, with its recommendation, to the Board of Managers.

SECT. 12. On all points not herein provided for, each section shall be governed by the charter, by-laws and usages of the Institute.

ARTICLE XII.—*Of Committees.*

SECTION 1. There shall be the following Standing Committees, each to consist of ten members, to be appointed by the President, at the first meeting after the annual election, who may be aided in his choice by nominations made at the annual meeting. All members notified of their appointment to any Committees, if they do not decline before the next stated meeting, shall be considered members thereof:—

1. On the Library.
2. On the Cabinet of Models.
3. On the Cabinet of Minerals and Geological Specimens.
4. On the Cabinet of Arts and Manufactures.
5. On Meteorology.
6. On Meetings.

SECT. 2. There shall be a Committee on Science and the Arts, which shall consist of forty-five (45) members of the Institute, to be elected as hereinafter prescribed, who shall pledge themselves by their acceptance of membership, to perform such duties as may devolve upon them and to sustain by their labors the scientific character of the Institute.

The Committee shall, within one month after the annual election of the Institute in each year, hold a meeting, at which they shall elect a Chairman. They may adopt rules for their government not inconsistent with the charter and by-laws of the Institute.

Special Committees to examine any subject shall be appointed by the Chairman, and shall make their reports in writing signed by the members thereof. A quorum for final action upon a report shall consist of not less than fifteen (15) members, and when such report is adopted it shall be accepted as the decision of the Institute.

It shall be the duty of the Chairman of the Committee to submit at the stated meetings of the Institute such action of the Committee as he may deem of interest to the Institute.

Applications for the examination of any subject shall be made to the Chairman of the Committee, either by the Institute or by the Secretary, who shall receive such application from inventors and others.

The members of the Committee shall be nominated at the stated meeting of the Institute in December, and shall be elected for three (3) years at the annual election—each year fifteen (15)—except that at the annual election in 1887 there shall be elected forty-five (45), who shall draw lots for terms of one (1), two (2) and three (3) years respectively.

The Committee shall report all vacancies occurring in their body, whether by neglect of duty or otherwise, to the stated meeting of the Institute next ensuing, at which such vacancies shall be filled.

The meetings of the Committee shall be open to all members of the Institute.

SECT. 3. Each of the Committees named in the first section shall choose, at their first meeting after their appointment, a Chairman.

The Committee on the Library, on Meetings, and on Science and Arts, shall meet at least once in each month, except in July and August ; the other Committees at the call of their Chairman.

Records of their proceedings shall be kept by the Secretary.

They shall report to the Institute, and shall be governed by such rules, not inconsistent with these by-laws, as may be adopted by them respectively. All Special Committees must report to the Institute in writing, at the next stated meeting succeeding their appointment, otherwise they may be considered discharged.

SECT. 4. No bills for expenses incurred by Committees shall be paid unless certified to by such Committee at a regular meeting, examined by the Auditors, and authorized by the Board of Managers,

ARTICLE XIII.—*Meetings.*

SECTION 1. The Institute shall hold stated meetings on the third Wednesday of each month, excepting in July and August. That on the third Wednesday in January of each year shall be styled the annual meeting.

SECT. 2. Special meetings shall be called by order of the President, upon request of the Board of Managers, or the written application of twelve members of the Institute. Fifteen members shall constitute a quorum.

ARTICLE XIV.—*Order of Business.*

SECTION 1. The stated meetings of the Institute shall be held at the hour of 8 o'clock, P. M.

SECT. 2. The order shall be as follows :—

1. Reading of the Minutes.
2. Reports from the Board of Managers.
3. Reports from Standing Committees, etc.
   (1) On the Library.
   (2) On the Cabinet of Minerals, etc.
   (3) On the Cabinet of Models.
   (4) On the Cabinet of Arts and Manufactures.
   (5) On Meteorology.
   (6) On Meetings.
   (7) On Science and the Arts.
   (8) The Curators.
4. Reports from Special Committees.
5. The paper announced for the evening.
6. The Secretary's report.
7. Deferred business.
8. Consideration of new business.

SECT. 3. At the annual meetings the reception of the report of the judges of the election shall always be in order.

SECT. 4. The order of business may be altered for any meeting by a vote of two-thirds of the members present thereat.

ARTICLE XV.—*Rules.*

The Institute, at its meetings, shall be governed by the following rules :—

First.—All resolutions must be presented in writing, signed by the mover, and must be seconded and announced by the Chair before consideration.

Second.—Any member rising to speak shall be announced by the Chair before proceeding.

Third.—The name of the mover of any resolution announced by the Chair shall be entered in the minutes.

Fourth.—No member shall be allowed to speak more than twice on any resolution, unless by special permission granted by the meeting, except he be the mover thereof, or the Chairman of the Committee reporting it, who shall have the privilege of closing the debate.

Fifth.—The yeas and nays shall be called at the request of five members. Each member attending any meeting of the Institute, shall, as he enters the Hall, report his name to the janitor, to be recorded in a book to be kept for the purpose.

Sixth.—The Chair shall decide whether any resolution does or does not pertain to the objects of the Institute; and in the latter case, shall decide it out of order, and from this decision there shall be no appeal.

Seventh.—Nominations for officers to be voted for at the annual meeting shall be made at the stated meeting in December, and the names of the nominees not declining shall be published, by posting in the Hall, thereafter until the election.

Eighth.—The first four rules hereinbefore stated, or either of them, may, by a vote of two-thirds of the members present at any meeting, be suspended for that meeting.

ARTICLE XVI.—*Board of Managers.*

SECTION 1. All the officers of the Institute, except the Auditors and Trustees, shall be, *ex-officio*, members of the Board of Managers, which shall have entire control of the current receipts and expenditures of the Institute. To the Board of Managers shall be confided all the business affairs of the Institute, not specially reserved to the Board of Trustees. The Board of Managers shall have authority to devise and execute all measures, not incompatible with the rights and duties of the Board of Trustees, which may, in their judgment, advance the interests of the Institute.

They shall have authority, by exchange, sale or otherwise, to add to or subtract from the collections of books, furniture and apparatus, in such manner, however, that the aggregate value of the same to the Institution, at any time, may not be impaired.

They shall have authority to elect members of the Institute, except Honorary and Corresponding Members, who shall be elected by the Institute.

SECT. 2. The Board of Managers shall keep regular minutes of their proceedings, which shall be open at all times to inspection by members of the Institute.

SECT. 3. The Board of Managers shall, at the annual meeting of the Institute, present a report of their proceedings and of the condition of the affairs of the Institute.

SECT. 4. They shall hold stated meetings once in each month. They shall select their own officers, except the Chairman, who shall be the President of the Institute, and in his absence, as provided for in Article VII, and shall be at liberty to make by-laws for their own regulation, not inconsistent with the charter, or with the by-laws of the Institute. Seven of their members shall constitute a quorum.

SECT. 5. All vacancies in the Board of Managers shall be filled at the next meeting of the Institute.

ARTICLE XVII.—*Amendments.*

Amendments to these by-laws, to be proposed at any stated meeting, shall be posted upon the notice-board by the first of the month. Such proposition, when presented to the meeting, may be considered, amended, referred, postponed, or rejected, or ordered to be published weekly in two or more daily papers published in the city of Philadelphia, by a majority vote.

At a subsequent stated meeting, after such publication, the amendment may be adopted by a vote of two-thirds of the members present, except in the case of Article II, relating to capital stock, which cannot be altered unless by a vote of a majority of the stock represented.

BY-LAWS OF THE BOARD OF MANAGERS.

SECTION 1. *Officers.*—The President of the Institute, or, in his absence, the Vice-President, in order of seniority of election, or in the absence of both, a member elected *pro tempore*, shall preside at all meetings of the Board. Records of its proceedings shall be kept by the Actuary.

SECT. 2. *Meetings.*—The Board shall hold a meeting for the purpose of organizing, appointing an Actuary, Standing Committees, etc., on the fourth Wednesday in January, and regular meetings on the second Wednesday of each month, at one o'clock, P. M.

SECT. 3. Special meetings may be called by the President whenever he shall deem the same necessary. In case of his absence or refusal to call a special meeting on the written request of five members of the Board of Managers, such special meeting shall be called by the Actuary.

SECT. 4. *Actuary.*—An Actuary shall be appointed by the Board at their first meeting after the annual election. He shall keep a correct record of their proceedings; keep a roll of the members, and note their attendance thereon ; give notice of all meetings of the Board, and of committees, by circulars, delivered at least two days prior to the day of meeting; act as Secretary of all Standing Committees of the Board ; notify all committees of the Board of their appointment, and transmit to the Chairman of each all papers or documents relating to the subject to be considered or acted upon. He shall collect and receive all moneys due to the Institute, and hand them over to the Treasurer ; shall act as agent of the *Journal* of the Institute, and shall transact such other business of the Institute as the Board shall direct. In all matters he shall be subject to the direction and control of the Board, and he shall be entitled to receive such yearly compensation as they may determine.

SECT. 5. *Resignations.*—All resignations of membership of the Board, after acceptance thereof, shall be reported to the Institute at its next stated meeting.

Members who have not attended six regular meetings prior to the stated meetings of the Institute in December, shall be reported thereat as having resigned, unless it be unanimously voted by the Board, at its stated meeting in December, that such member has been absent for sufficient reason.

SECT. 6. *Standing Committees.*—The following Standing Committees, consisting of five members each, shall be appointed by the President and approved by the Board :—

1. On Instruction. 2. On Election and Resignation of Members. 3. On Stocks and Finance. 4. On Publications. 5. On Exhibitions. 6. On Sectional Arrangements.

It shall be the duty of these committees to keep regular minutes of their proceedings, and report them monthly to the Board, and to report to the stated meeting of the Board in December an estimate of moneys they require for the service of the ensuing year.

SECT. 7. *Curators.*—Two members of the Board shall be selected at their first meeting after the annual election, to serve as curators for the ensuing year and until their successors shall be appointed. They shall have charge of all the property of the Institute, except such records, papers and books as may be assigned to the officers. They shall keep regular minutes of their proceedings, and report the same to the Board at its regular meetings.

SECT. 8. *Professorships.*—There shall be Professors of Chemistry, Natural Philosophy, Mechanics, and other departments, as the Board of Managers may direct, to be elected by the Board annually for a term of one year, at its first meeting after the annual election, and to receive such compensation as the Board may, from time to time, determine. The professors shall be, *ex-officio*, members of the Committee on Instruction, in addition to the five members named in Section 6.

SECT. 9. *Order of Business.*—The order at the stated meetings shall be as follows :—

1. Calling the roll.
2. Reading the minutes and action thereon.
3. Report from Treasurer, and action on bills.
4. Reports from Standing Committees and action thereon.
    (*a.*) On Instruction.
    (*b.*) On Election and Resignation of Members.
    (*c.*) On Stocks and Finance.
    (*d.*) On Publications.
    (*e.*) On Exhibitions.
    (*f.*) On Sectional Arrangements.
5. Reports from Special Committees and action thereon.
6. Reading correspondence.
7. Donations.
8. Deferred business.
9. New business.
10. Excuses for non-attendance and action thereon.
11. Calling the roll.

SECT. 10. *Amendments.*—These by-laws may be altered at any stated meeting of the Board, provided the alteration be approved by two-thirds of the members present.

SECT. 11. A suitable person shall be appointed by the Secretary to act as janitor, with the approval of the Board, who may be discharged by the Secretary for misconduct.

REGULATIONS OF THE COMMITTEE ON SCIENCE AND THE ARTS

Approved by the Institute at the stated meeting held June 21, 1893, and adopted at the stated meeting of the Committee on Science and the Arts, held September 6, 1893.

MEETINGS.

1. The Committee shall hold stated meetings at 8 o'clock P. M. on the first Wednesday of each month, excepting July and August. Special meetings may be called by the Chairman, and shall be called by him upon the written request of five members of the Committee.

2. At all meetings of the Committee nine members shall constitute a quorum, except that a quorum for final action upon a report shall consist of not less than fifteen members.

CHAIRMAN.

1. Nominations for Chairman to serve for one year shall be made at the stated meeting of the Committee in February, and the election shall be by ballot at the same meeting, and the person receiving the highest number of votes shall be declared elected. The Chairman shall hold his office until his successor shall be installed. He shall not be eligible for election for two successive terms.

2. He shall take the chair at the hour appointed, preserve order and decorum in debate, suppress all personal reflections, and confine the remarks of members to the question under discussion. When two or more members rise at the same time, he shall designate the one entitled to the floor.

3. He shall decide all questions of order. An appeal from his decision to the Committee cannot be made by less than two members. He may, however, submit questions of order to the Committee for their decision.

4. On questions of order, there shall be no debate, except on an appeal from the decision of the Chairman, or on a reference of a question by him to the Committee. On questions of order, no member shall speak more than once, unless by leave of the Committee; on other questions, a member may speak twice, but not oftener, without leave.

5. The Chairman shall appoint the members of all sub-committees, unless otherwise ordered, but shall not serve on any such sub-committee; and whenever he shall ascertain that any member of a sub-committee is absent, or fails to discharge the duties assigned to him, he is empowered to substitute another.

ORDER OF BUSINESS.

1. Calling the roll.
2. Reading of the minutes of the preceding meeting.
3. Reading of correspondence.
4. Reports on applications, and consideration thereof.
5. Consideration of reports for final action.
6. Reports of sub-committees, first reading.
7. Deferred business.
8. New business.
9. Calling the roll.
10. Adjournment.

INVESTIGATIONS.

1. It shall be competent for the Committee at all times, by vote of a majority of the members present, to investigate by sub-committee any subject which shall be presented on the motion of a member, and to remit the usual charge for investigation.

2. Every inventor or other person who may submit a subject to the Committee for investigation, shall be furnished by the Secretary with a copy of the rules and regulations of the Committee governing investigations.

3. The party desiring investigation of any subject shall make a written request addressed to the Committee, and upon receiving notice from the Secretary that his application has been accepted, he shall deposit with the Secretary the sum of five dollars to cover the ordinary cost of investigation and report.

4. All applications for investigations addressed to the Committee shall first be referred to a special committee to be appointed by the Chairman, styled the "Committee on Preliminary Examination," the membership of which shall be known only to the Chairman and Secretary. It shall be the duty of the Committee on Preliminary Examination to pass judgment on the character of applications referred to them, and, at each stated meeting, to submit a report of their work, recommending as worthy of investigation such applications as in their judgment are meritorious, and as unworthy such as they may judge to be unimportant.

5. No person shall be a member of a sub-committee of investigation who is or has been interested in the issue, either pecuniarily or as counsel for the applicant.

6. All members of a sub-committee making a report, whether members of the general Committee or not, shall receive notice of any meetings at which said report will be considered, and shall have the right to the floor in the discussion thereof, and the Secretary shall state this fact on the notices of appointment of members of sub-committees.

7. A quorum for the transaction of business at any meeting of a sub-committee properly called, shall consist of the member or members present, irrespective of numbers.

8. No inventor or other person interested in the issue of an investigation shall be present at a meeting of a sub-committee or of the general Committee, when the merits of a subject or invention in which he is interested shall be under discussion, except at the invitation of the sub-committee charged with the investigation; but after the report of the sub-committee has passed first reading, he may examine it, on application to the Secretary, and may make any explanations or objections, in writing, addressed to the Chairman of the general Committee; *provided*, that such explanations or objections shall be submitted not latter than the next stated meeting of the general Committee.

9. No subject, or invention, can be withdrawn after it has been assigned to a sub-committee for investigation without the consent of the general Committee.

10. Sub-committees in preparing their reports shall accompany them with drawings or diagrams, whenever these will serve to illustrate the subject of their reports; and they shall be authorized, whenever they shall think it necessary, to require inventors, or other persons interested in the investigations, to furnish such drawings or diagrams as a condition of their making such investigations and reports.

Reports on all subjects must be signed by a majority of those members of the sub-committee who have participated in the investigations. Minority reports may be received and considered by a vote of the majority of the members present. When a report is issued, it shall have attached to it the names of the Chairman and Secretary.

11. When any sub-committee deems the subject upon which it reports worthy of an award of the Certificate of Merit, the Edward Longstreth Medal of Merit, the John Scott Legacy Premium and Medal, or the Elliott Cresson Medal, it shall append to its report a recommendation to that effect, and such recommendation shall not be

changed by the general Committee, except by a vote of two-thirds of the members present.

It shall not be competent for any member of the Committee on Science and the Arts to be a competitor for any of the medals or other awards in the gift or subject to the recommendation of the said Committee, unless the subject for award be referred to the Committee for examination by a vote of the Institute.

12. The reports of all sub-committees may be discussed at the meeting of the general Committee at which they are first presented, but shall be laid over for second reading and final action until the next meeting, except that, by unanimous vote of the members present, they may be taken up for second reading and finally disposed of.

13. It shall be the duty of the Secretary to certify to the applicant the action of the Committee, and to furnish one copy of its report within ten days after the same shall have been finally adopted, except in cases where the Committee has made or recommended an award, when the copy shall be withheld from the applicant and from publication during the time in which proper objections to such award, or motion for reconsideration, may be made. In default of such motion or objections, the previous action upon a report and award shall be final.

14. After a report has been finally acted on it shall not be reconsidered, except by a vote of two-thirds of the members present. A motion for reconsideration must be made not later than the next stated meeting after the adoption of the report which it is proposed to reconsider, and may be acted on at the next following stated meeting. After a report has been finally acted on a second investigation of the same subject-matter shall not be ordered, except on a vote of two-thirds of the members present.

15. After the second roll-call at each meeting the Secretary shall report the name of every member who has been absent from three successive stated meetings, and has not during that time attended a meeting of a sub-committee, and unless otherwise severally ordered by a vote of a majority of the members present, each such member shall be considered as having resigned.

16. These regulations may be altered in the following manner : Propositions for amendment shall be made at a stated meeting in writing. They may be considered when presented, but shall not be acted on until the next stated meeting, and shall be considered adopted when agreed to by two-thirds of the members present. In all cases, notice of proposed amendments shall be given by publication on card notices.

CERTIFICATE OF MERIT.

The following is published for information (Extract from the minutes of the stated meeting of the Franklin Institute, held Wednesday, June 21, 1882) :—

At the stated meeting of the Institute, held on the above date, the following resolutions were adopted :—

" *Resolved*, That the Committee on Science and the Arts of the Franklin Institute is hereby authorized to award, and issue to persons by said Committee adjudged worthy, a Certificate of Merit for their inventions, discoveries or productions, which Certificate shall read as follows :—

" The FRANKLIN INSTITUTE of the State of Pennsylvania for the promotion of the Mechanic Arts, awards to ———— this Certificate of Merit. This award is made pursuant to the recommendation of the Committee on Science and the Arts.

" Report No.————   Approved, ————— 18—

" Chairman Committee Science and the Arts.

" ———————— President.

[SEAL.]   " ———————— Secretary.

" *Resolved*, That all such Certificates of Merit so awarded shall be signed by the President and Secretary of the Franklin Institute and he Chairman of the Committee on Science and the Arts, and attested by the seal of the Institute, and be transmitted to the person named therein by the Secretary."

The Committee on Science and the Arts has adopted general regulations on investigations, which govern the award of the Certificate of Merit ; see Regulations Nos. 11, 13 and 14.

(An award of the Certificate of Merit requires no advertisement.)

The following resolutions were adopted at the stated meeting of the Institute, held January 16, 1895 :—

" *Resolved*, That the Institute issue diplomas to applicants in cases where awards of medals have been made to inventors, and where the applicants have failed to receive recognition for their share in the development of an invention.

" *Resolved*, That in order to further increase the value of awards, as well as to give greater publicity to the work of the Committee on Science and the Arts, each such award or recommendation shall be accompanied by an engraved certificate of the fact suitable for framing."

THE EDWARD LONGSTRETH MEDAL OF MERIT.

The following is a brief history of this endowment :—

In the month of May, 1890, Edward Longstreth, machinist, and retired member of the Baldwin Locomotive Works of the city of Philadelphia, deposited with the Franklin Institute, in trust, a registered bond of the Baltimore Traction Co. for the sum of one thousand dollars, for the founding and perpetuation of the Edward Longstreth Silver Medal ; the interest accruing from said principal sum to be used in procuring and awarding said medals for the encouragement of invention, and in recognition of meritorious work in science and the industrial arts ; the said awards to be made by the Franklin Institute through its Committee on Science and the Arts, under such rules as said Committee may adopt.

This donor further presented to the Franklin Institute twelve silver medals and the dies therefor designed and executed under the direction of a Committee of the Institute with the approval of the donor.

The observe of the medal bears the effigy of the donor, and is inscribed around the margin, " The Edward Longstreth Medal of Merit, founded 1890." On the reverse is inscribed around the margin, " Awarded by the Franklin Institute," the centre to be filled by the engraved name of the recipient, with the object of award and date.

On May 14, 1890, the Board of Managers of the Franklin Institute, by resolution, accepted on behalf of the Institute the gifts of the donor, and on September 17, 1890, the Institute, by the resolution following, confirmed the acceptance :—

" *Resolved*, That the Institute hereby confirms the action of the Board of Managers in accepting the gift of foundation of the EDWARD LONGSTRETH MEDAL OF MERIT, and in expressing its grateful acknowledgments for the gift.

" *Resolved*, That the grant of the Edward Longstreth Medal, in accordance with the wishes of the donor, be entrusted to the Committee on Science and the Arts, subject to such conditions as the said Committee, with the approval of the Institute, may propose."

In conformity with the foregoing instructions, the Committee on Science and the Arts has established the following rules to be observed in awarding the Edward Longstreth Medal of Merit :—

" 1. This medal may be awarded for useful invention, important discovery, and meritorious work in, or contributions to, science, or the industrial arts.

" 2. In all cases where the subject of investigation shall be judged worthy of the award of the Edward Longstreth Medal of Merit, the adoption of the report containing such an award by the Committee on Science and the Arts shall be conclusive without advertisement as required in the case of other awards by the Committee.

"3. In the event of an accumulation of the fund for medals beyond the sum of one hundred dollars, it shall be competent for the Committee on Science and the Arts to offer from such surplus a money premium for some special work on any mechanical or scientific subject that said Committee may consider of sufficient importance."

At the stated meeting of the Franklin Institute, held Wednesday, January 21, 1891, the Secretary, by direction of the Committee on Science and the Arts, presented the report of this Committee in reference to the regulations for the grant of the Edward Longstreth Medal of Merit. On motion, the Committee's action was confirmed, and the regulations proposed in the report were approved.

The Committee on Science and the Arts has adopted general regulations on investigations which govern the award of the Edward Longstreth Medal of Merit ; see Regulations Nos. 11, 13 and 14.

(An award of the Edward Longstreth Medal requires no advertisement.)

THE JOHN SCOTT LEGACY PREMIUM AND MEDAL.

The following particulars are published for the information of the ingenious :—

John Scott, chemist, late of Edinburgh, by his will, made in the year 1816, bequeathed the sum of four thousand dollars in the funded three per cent. stock of the United States, to the corporation of the city of Philadelphia, directing that the interest and dividend to be come receivable thereon should be laid out in premiums, to be distributed among ingenious men and women who make useful inventions, but no such premium to exceed twenty dollars, and that therewith shall be given a copper medal with this inscription : " To the most deserving."

The Select and Common Councils of the city of Philadelphia, by an ordinance passed February 27, 1834, vested the award of the aforesaid premiums and medals in the Franklin Institute of the State of Pennsylvania for the promotion of the Mechanic Arts.

The Legislature of the State of Pennsylvania, by an act passed and approved June 30, 1869, created a " Board of Directors of City Trusts," to whom was referred the charge or administration of all estates dedicated to charitable uses.

The control of the John Scott Legacy Premium and Medal was (by the Act of 1869) transferred to the Board of Directors of City Trusts.

This Board, by a resolution passed April 12, 1882, referred the matter, with instructions, to their Committee on Wills' Hospital and Minor Trusts.

The Committee on Wills' Hospital and Minor Trusts, by a resolution passed April 12, 1882, resolved that "they will favorably receive the names of any persons whom the Franklin Institute may from time to time report to the Committee on Minor Trusts as worthy of receiving the John Scott Legacy Medal and Premium."

The Franklin Institute, by a resolution passed June 21, 1882, accepted the above, and referred the duty of making examinations, etc., to the Committee on Science and the Arts.

That Committee has adopted the following rules in regard to recommendations of the award of the John Scott Legacy Premium and Medal :—

1. A recommendation for an award of the premium and medal shall only be made by the Committee on Science and the Arts, on a report of a sub-committee, which shall have been appointed to examine such invention.

2. The invention or improvement to be examined shall be accompanied by a clear description and drawings of the same, together with a model, if required, and also a statement of the particulars of the inventor's claim to originality.

3. When the invention is a composition of matter, specimens of the ingredients and of the compound sufficient for the purpose of experiments, and to preserve in the cabinet of the Franklin Institute, shall be furnished by the inventor.

4. Upon the adoption by the Committee on Science and the Arts of a report setting forth that an invention or improvement is worthy of an award of the premium and medal, publication shall be made three times in the Journal of the Franklin Institute, stating that at the expiration of three months from the date of the first publication, the Committee on Science and the Arts will recommend to the Committee on Minor Trusts of the Board of City Trusts, the award of the said premium and medal to the inventor, unless within that time satisfactory evidence shall have been submitted to the Committee on Science and the Arts of the want of originality of the supposed invention and improvement. In case no objections to the final award of the premium and medal shall have been made, the Secretary shall certify the recommendation of the award to the Committee on Minor Trusts of the Board of City Trusts.

5. All applications for the John Scott Legacy Premium and Medal must be made to the Secretary of the Institute, by whom the applications and accompanying descriptions, drawings, etc., shall be laid

before the Committee on Science and the Arts, and by whom all publications ordered by said Committee, in relation to said premiums and
medals, shall be made.

THE ELLIOTT CRESSON MEDAL.

[ABSTRACT OF THE DEED OF TRUST.]

Under date of February 18, 1848, Elliott Cresson, Esq., of Philadelphia, Pennsylvania, conveyed to Trustees, for the Franklin Institute,
one thousand dollars of the six per cent. convertible loan of the President, Managers and Company of the Schuylkill Navigation Company
—to hold the said sum and the interest to accrue thereon, for the
following use and purposes :—

1. The Trustees to keep the principal invested as it now is until it
is reimbursed by the said Company, and immediately after such
reimbursement to reinvest the said principal of one thousand dollars
in such securities, bearing interest, as may by law be designated for
the investment of trust funds. And from time to time, as the said
principal sum may be reimbursed, reinvest the same in like manner.

2. To cause suitable dies to be prepared for striking the gold
medal out of the first sufficient moneys received for interest on the said
sum of one thousand dollars. The dies to bear the following devices
and inscriptions: The obverse—a medallion likeness of the said
Elliott Cresson, with inscription around the margin, " Elliott Cresson
Medal, A. D. 1848." Reverse—around the margin, "Awarded by the
Franklin Institute of Pennsylvania." The centre to be filled by engrav-
ing the name of the party to whom awarded and the year in which the
award may be made.

3. After the said dies have been prepared, and paid for out of the
money received for interest, the said Trustees to cause to be struck from
time to time such number of gold medals as the interest received will
pay for, and deliver the same to the Treasurer of the Franklin Institute, to be by him delivered to such persons or parties as the said
Franklin Institute, by any rule or regulation they may adopt, may have
awarded the same. The said awards, however, to be in all instances
made either for some discovery in the arts and sciences, or for the
invention or improvement of some useful machine, or for some new
process or combination of materials in manufactures, or for ingenuity,
skill or perfection in workmanship.

At the stated meeting of the Institute held May 17, 1849—On
motion, it was

Resolved, That the Committee on Science and the Arts be authorized
to award the Elliott Cresson Medal to such inventions and manufactures

as shall, in their opinion, deserve it, subject to the rules which now
govern the award of the John Scott Legacy Premium and Medal.
(Repealed at the stated meeting held September 20, 1893.)

At the stated meeting held September 20, 1893, the following reso·
lution was adopted :—

Resolved, That the Committee on Science and the Arts be authorized to award the Elliott Cresson Medal for such discoveries, inventions
or manufactures as shall, in their opinion, deserve it, subject to the
general regulations on investigations and the following special rules :—

1. Upon the adoption, by the Committee on Science and the Arts,
of a report setting forth that an invention or improvement is worthy of
an award of the Elliott Cresson Medal, publication shall be made three
times in the Journal of the Franklin Institute, stating that at the expiration of three months from the date of the first publication, the applicant will be entitled to receive the award of the said medal, unless
within that time satisfactory evidence shall have been submitted to the
Committee on Science and the Arts of the want of originality of the
supposed discovery, invention or improvement.

2. All applications for the Elliott Cresson Medal must be made
to the Secretary of the Institute, by whom the applications and accompanying descriptions, drawings, etc., shall be laid before the Committee
on Science and the Arts, and by whom all publications ordered by said
Committee, in relation to said medal, shall be made.

DRAWING SCHOOL.

The sessions of the Drawing School are divided into two courses, viz. :—

A Winter Term of fifteen weeks, beginning about the middle of September and ending in the second week of January.

A Spring Term of fifteen weeks, beginning about the middle of January and ending about the close of April.

Thorough instruction, based upon the most modern and approved practice, is given in Mechanical, Architectural and Free-hand Drawing. Admittance to the lectures of the Institute is free to the scholars on Friday evenings.

The class rooms open at 7 P. M. on Tuesday and Thursday evenings. Instruction commences at 7.15 and ends at 9.15 P. M.

The school is divided into the following classes :—

JUNIOR CLASS, in which drawing tools and their proper manipulation, lines, surfaces, and single solids with plain surfaces are treated.

All students are advised to go through these classes, in order thoroughly to understand the principles of drawing, before entering the senior or architectural class.

INTERMEDIATE CLASS, in which solids with curved surfaces, the intersections of solids, and the development of their surfaces are treated.

SENIOR CLASS, in which the methods, technicalities, and style of drawing and designing engineering work are treated.

ARCHITECTURAL CLASS, in which designs, plans, elevations, and details of buildings, and of interior and ornamental work are treated.

FREE-HAND CLASS, in which free-hand drawing with pencil and crayon from the flat and from casts, designing and oil painting, are treated.

That more efficient and rapid progress may be made, the Director has prepared text-books on Mechanical Drawing, with plates, which can be purchased at the class rooms, together with all necessary tools and materials.

Each student is required to provide himself with tools and materials.

The full course comprises four terms, at the end of which certifi cates are awarded to those students who have shown sufficient attention, industry and progress.

Annual announcement is made of the times of opening and closing the school terms, price of tuition, etc., copies of which may be obtained at the office of the Actuary.

SCHEDULE OF MEETINGS, ETC.

First Wednesday of each month (except July and August), 8 P. M.,
COMMITTEE ON SCIENCE AND THE ARTS.

Second Wednesday of each month, I P. M.,
BOARD OF MANAGERS.

Third Tuesday of each month (except July and August), 8 P. M.,
CHEMICAL SECTION.

Third Wednesday of each month (except July and August), 8 P. M.,
INSTITUTE.

Fourth Tuesday of each month (except July and August), 8 P. M.,
ELECTRICAL SECTION.

Friday Evenings (8 o'clock) of the months of November to March,
inclusive .... LECTURES.

Membership tickets admit to all stated meetings and lectures.
Visitors invited or accompanied by members have the privilege of
attending the stated meetings of the Institute.

HISTORICAL RELICS—MODELS, ETC.'

Among the acquisitions of the Institute, valuable or interesting for their historic associations, the following may be named:—

The dress sword of Dr. Franklin, worn by him while representing the United States at the Court of France. This interesting relic was presented to the Institute by R. Meade Bache. It is deposited with the Historical Society of Pennsylvania.

A cylinder electrical machine, once the property of Dr. Franklin. Presented by Dr. John Redman Coxe, of Philadelphia.

Machine for dressing type, formerly the property of Dr. Franklin. Presented by Prof. Franklin Bache.

Several pieces of electrical apparatus, believed to have been owned by Dr. Franklin. Presented by Dr. W. Ruschenberger, of Philadelphia.

Odométre, formerly belonging to Dr. Franklin, and, later, to Thomas Jefferson. Presented by Wm. McFarland, Richmond, Va.

Portrait of Dr. Franklin, painted by Thomas Sully. Presented by him.

Medallion of Dr. Franklin, executed in France, dated 1777. Presented by Dr. J. L. Sharpless, of Philadelphia.

Copy of Reaumur's L'Art de Convertir le Fer Forgé en Acier, 1772, bearing Franklin's autograph.

Portfolio of prints of metal house-furnishing goods, formerly belonging to Dr. Franklin. Presented by J. D.'Sergeant, Philadelphia.

A considerable collection of letters, memorandum and note-books, of Oliver Evans. Deposited by Oliver Evans Wood, of Philadelphia, 1894.

Model of Oliver Evans' "Columbian" high-pressure steam engine. Made by Rush & Muhlenberg. Presented by S. J. Robbins, July 18, 1833.

Magneto-electric machine. Made by Joseph Saxton. Exhibited at the meeting of the British Association in 1833.

Model of the Redheffer "perpetual motion." Made and presented by Isaiah Lukens. (This model possesses special interest. It was built for the purpose of exposing the fraudulent nature of the claim of Chas. H. Redheffer to have discovered a self-acting machine ; for the investigation of which the' Legislature of Pennsylvania, in 1812, appointed a commission of experts).

Autograph of George Stephenson, with drawing in his own hand of the first locomotive tender devised by him. Presented by James B. Winslow, on behalf of the Boston and Lowell Railroad Company, 1872,

Model of George Stephenson's "No. 1" locomotive, built for the Stockton and Darlington Railroad. Brought from England by Wm. Strickland in 1826, and by him presented.

Portrait of Daguerre, painted by Abraham Whiteside. Presented by Mrs. F. O. Willard, of Philadelphia.

Godfrey's quadrant, original model. Made by James Ham, Jr., Philadelphia, September 10, 1781. Deposited by Dr. Chas. M. Wetherill, May 4, 1852.

Unfinished bust of Henry Clay (wood carving), by Wm. Rush. Presented by Samuel Richards.

Early Morse printer. Deposited by James Swaim, of Philadelphia.

Autograph sketch of a "break detecter," by Prof. Morse (bearing his signature). Presented on behalf of The New York Electrical Society, by James D. Reid, December 1, 1887.

Minute-book and seal of the first telegraph company. Deposited by Joseph Sailer, Jr., Philadelphia, 1885.

COMPLETE SETS OF SERIALS.

The folowing partial list of complete sets, selected with the view of embracing the greatest variety of subjects, will give a fair idea of the extent and condition of this class of reference literature in the library :—

(AMERICAN).

American Agriculturist.
American Architect and Building News.
American Association for the Advancement of Science, Proceedings.
American Chemical Journal.
American Chemical Society, Journal.
American Exchange and Review.
American Gas Light Journal.
American Institute of Electrical Engineers, Transactions.
American Institute of Mining Engineers, Transactions.
American Journal of Pharmacy.
American Journal of Mathematics.
American Journal of Science.
American Naturalist.
American Pharmaceutical Association, Proceedings.
American Society of Civil Engineers, Proceedings and Transactions.
American Society of Mechanical Engineers, Transactions.
Electrical Engineer.
Electrical World.
Encyclopedias.—American, and Annuals.
Britannica (American edition).
Chambers' (American edition).
Johnson's.
Rees'.
Engineering Magazine.
Engineering News.
Franklin Institute, Journal.
Manufacturer and Builder.
Mathematical Monthly.
Official Gazette of the United States Patent Office.
Poor's Manual of Railroads.
Popular Science Monthly.

Railroad Gazette.
Sanitarian.
Scientific American (Architects' and Builders' edition).
Scientific American, Supplement.
Smithsonian Institution. Contributions to Knowledge, Miscella-
neous Collection, Special Reports.
Specifications and Drawings of Patents. United States.
Textile Colorist.
United States Coast Survey Charts.
United States Hydrographic Office Charts.
United States Naval Institute, Proceedings.

(BRITISH).

Australasian Association for the Advancement of Science, Reports.
British Association for the Advancement of Science, Reports.
Builder.
Chemical News.
Chemical Society, Journal.
Electrical Review (Telegraphic Journal).
Engineer.
Engineering.
Geological Society of London, Quarterly Journal.
Illustrated Official Journal. (Patents).
Institution of Civil Engineers, Proceedings.
Institution of Electrical Engineers, Journal.
Institution of Mechanical Engineers, Proceedings.
Institution of Naval Architects, Transactions.
Iron and Steel Institute, Journal.
Journal of Gas Lighting.
Journal of Science. (Quarterly.)
London, Edinburgh and Dublin Philosophical Magazine, (inclu-
ding Nicholson, Tilloch, Thompson, Jamieson, Brewster).
Mechanics' Magazine, (including Iron, Industries and Industries
and Iron).
Nature.
Photographic News.
Repertory of Arts and Sciences. (Newton's).
Royal Society. Catalogue of Scientific Papers, Proceedings,
Transactions.
Society of Arts, Journal.
Society of Chemical Industry, Journal.
Specifications of Inventions. (British Patent Reports).

(FRENCH).

Académie des Sciences, Comptes Rendus.
Annales des Mines.
"   "   Ponts et Chausées.
"   "   Travaux Publics.
"   Industrielles.
Association Française pour l'Avancement des Sciences, Comptes
    Rendus.
Brevets d'Invention.
Conservatoire des Arts et Métiers, Annales.
Électricien.
La Lumière Électrique.
La Nature.
Nouvelles Annales de la Construction.
Portefeuille Economique des Machines.
Publication Industrielle, Armengaud.
Revue Général de l'Architecture.
Revue Général de Chemin de Fer.
Société d'Encouragement pour l'Industrie Nationale, Bulletin.

(GERMAN).

Annalen der Chemie und Pharmacie (Liebig et al).
Annalen der Physik und Chemie (Wiedemann).
Chemiker Zeitung.
Deutsche Chemische Gesellschaft, Berichte.
Dingler's Polytechnisches Journal.
Elektrotechnische Bibliothek.
Elektrotechnische Zeitschrift.
Jahresberichte: Berzelius, Liebig und Kopp u. A., Städel, Wagner,
    Fischer.
Journal für Gasbeleuchtung.
Journal für Praktische Chemie.
Patent Blatt.
Repertorium der Analytischen Chemie.
Société Industrielle de Mulhouse, Bulletin.
Stahl und Eisen.
Verein Deutscher Ingenieure, Zeitschrift.
Verein zur Beförderung des Gewerbefleisses, Zeitschrift.
Zeitschrift für Analytische Chemie.
Zeitschrift für Berg-Huetten-und Salinen-Wesen im Preussischen
    Staate.

MEMBERS OF THE BOARD OF MANAGERS.

1824-1895.

WITH TERM OF SERVICE.

Abbot, William. 1824–1826.
Agnew, John. 1831–1863.
Addicks, John E. 1845–1850.
Allen, James. 1845.
Archer, Ellis S. 1858–1859.
Allison, William C. 1863.
Adamson, William. 1864.

Browne, Peter A. 1824–1827.
Beck, Jr., Paul. 1824–1827.
Biddle, Clement C. 1824.
Beale, Joseph. 1827.
Bolton, James M. 1830.
Bache, Alexander Dallas. 1830–1844.
Bulkley, James H. 1830–1841.
Betts, William C. 1844.
Burtis, Aaron H. 1845.
Birkinbine, Henry P. M. 1851–1856.
Baldwin, Matthias W. 1827–1863.
Barras, Joseph J. 1851–1860.
Baugh, Harman. 1855.
Bryson, James H. 1857–1863.
Bartol, Barnabas H. 1863–1865.
Briggs, Robert. 1864, and 1867–1873.
Bement, William B. 1866–1870.
Bement, Clarence S. 1871.
Bullock, Charles. 1868 to present time.
Birkbeck, John. 1869–1871.
Bartol, Henry W. 1870–1878.
Bergner, Theodore. 1870–1875.
Barker, George F. 1874–1875.
Banes, Charles H. 1877 to present time.
Burnham, George. 1878.
Bilgram, Hugo. 1885–1890.

Bower, Henry. 1891 to present time.
Beardsley, Arthur. 1894 to present time.

Carey, Mathew. 1824–1828.
Clarke, James. 1824–1826.
Cloud Joseph. 1824.
Collins, Isaac. 1828.
Cresson, John C. 1835–1863.
Carr, William Hart. 1837–1845.
Cresson, William P. 1848–1849.
Copper, John C. 1851.
Conarroe, George W. 1851–1863.
Cornelius, Robert. 1855–1863.
Cramp, Charles H. 1864–1867 and 1875 and 1895 to present time.
Chase, Pliny E. 1864–1886.
Close, Charles S. 1865–1879.
Cartwright, Henry. 1865–1881.
Cornelius, Robert C. 1866–1868.
Cooper, John H. 1870–1873.
Chambers, Jr., Cyrus. 1876–1890.
Chabot, Cyprien. 1877.
Cresson, George V. 1886 to present time.
Codman, John E. 1892–1894.
Conard, Thomas P. 1894 to present time.

Donaldson, Joseph. 1825.
Draper, Edmund. 1847–1850.
Dougherty, James. 1858–1861.
Drown, William A. 1861–1863.
Dreer, Ferdinand J. 1862.
Divine, William. 1864.
Durfee, William F. 1872–1873.
DuBois, William L. 1880–1882.
Darrach, Charles G. 1894 to present time.

Eisenhut, John D. 1824–1825.
Emerson, G. 1828.
Eastwick, Andrew M. 1836–1844.
Evans, Owen. 1844–1857.
Ellis, James P. 1848–1851.
Eckert, Geo. M. 1852–1854.
Erety, George. 1854–1866.
Eastwick, Edward P. 1859–1860.
Eldridge, G. Morgan. 1885–1890.

Fletcher, Thomas. 1824–1850.
Fry, William. 1825.
Fox, George. 1828–1830.
Fraley, Frederick. 1829–1863 and 1865–1882.
Ferguson, Alexander. 1831–1841.
Fling, William B. 1842.
Frazer, John F. 1844–1866.
Farr, George W. 1851.
Frazer, Persifor. 1880–1891.

Gilpin, Thomas. 1824.
Groves, Daniel. 1824–1827.
Garrigues, Isaac B. 1825–1863.
Griffith, Robert E. 1827.
Gobrecht, Christian. 1828–1830.
Gilder, John. 1838–1841.
Greble, Edwin. 1841–1863.
Graff, Frederick. 1852–1854 and 1858–1865 and 1880–1890.
Gries, John M. 1858–1862.
Gardiner, John., Jr. 1864.
Griffith R. Egglesfield. 1870–1871.
Garrison, F. Lynwood. 1890 to present time.
Gibson, J. Howard. 1893–1894.

Harrison, John. 1824–1829.
Horn, Henry. 1824.
Haviland, John. 1824–1826.
Harper, James. 1824–1826.
Humphreys, Samuel. 1826.
Hansell, William S. 1827.
Hays, Isaac. (M. D.) 1828–1841.
Harker, Joshua G. 1831–1836.
Hufty, Samuel. 1834–1850.
Hutchison, James. 1841–1842.
Hand, James C. 1845–1846.
Herse, George P.. 1851.
Harrison, Jos., Jr. 1854 and 1856–1859.
Howard, George C. 1855–1858.
Harris, William. 1860–1863.

Hutchinson, Joseph. 1860–1863.
Harding, George. 1864–1865.
Hunter, James. 1864.
Horstman, William J. 1865–1868.
Hart, Samuel. 1865–1870.
Helme, William. 1869–1888.
Houston, Edwin, J. 1874 to present time.
Heller, Charles S. 1879–1880.
Heyl, Henry R. 1879 to present time.
Hutchinson, Charles H. 1888–1890.
Harrison, Alfred C. 1895 to present time.

Jones, Thomas P. 1826–1828.
Johnson, Lawrence. 1855–1859.
Jones, Washington. 1859 to present time.
Jayne, Harry W. 1891 to present time.

Keating, William H. 1824–1826 and 1830–1840.
Katez, I. 1824.
Kneass, William. 1825.
Kirk, Charles H. 1830.
Knight, Daniel R. 1845.
King, Robert P. 1850.
Kelly, Henry H. 1851.
Knight, Jacob B. 1875–1879.

Lukens, Isaiah. 1824–1825 and 1828–1846.
Lewis, Harvey. 1824–1827.
Lewis, Mordecai D. 1828–1836.
Loud, Thomas. 1829–1831.
Lindsay, Robert. 1834–1836.
Linnard, James M. 1836–1838.
Lindsay, John. 1843.
Love, William H. 1859.
LeVan, W. Barnet. 1864–1876.
Longstreth, Edward. 1868–1870 and 1887 to present time.
Lewis, Enoch. 1868–1894.
Linville, J. Hayes. 1868.
Lucas, John. 1888–1894.

Merrick, Samuel V. 1824–1863.
Mason, David H. 1824.
Miller, Abraham. 1824–1858.
McAlpin, James, 1825–1828.
Mifflin, Lloyd. 1825–1826.

McEuen, Thomas. (M. D.) 1829.
McClurg, Alexander. 1833–1839.
Morris, Isaac P. 1836–1843.
Morris, Ellwood. 1844–1847.
Morris, William E. 1847–1851.
McClure, John. 1853–1856.
Megargee, Charles. 1858.
Moore, Joseph W. 1860–1861.
Mason, James S. 1861.
Merrick, J. Vaughan. 1864–1884.
Mitchell, William A. 1864–1865.
Moore, Bloomfield H. 1864–1876.
Morris, Henry G. 1864–1879.
Morton, Henry. 1865–1870.
Miles, Frederick B. 1874.
Mitchell, J. E. 1874 and 1876–1887.
McCambridge, Richard. 1876.
Marshall, Samuel R. 1887–1883.
McKean, William V. 1879–1883.
Marks, William D. 1881–1884.
Mucklé, M. Richards, Jr. 1894 to present time.

Newhall, Paul W. 1843–1844.
Naylor, Jacob. 1863 and 1865–1872.
Neafie, Jacob G. 1868.
Norris, Isaac. (M. D.) 1870–1881 and 1882 to present time.
Nystrom, John W. 1873–1875.

O'Neill, John. 1827–1832.
Ogden, John M. 1833.
Ogle, Williams. 1845–1850.
Orr, Hector. 1871–1887.
Outerbridge, Alex. E., Jr. 1881–1886.

Patterson, Robert. 1824.
Patterson, Robert M. 1825–1827.
Perot, William S. 1833–1834.
Parrish, William D. 1838 and 1852–1854.
Palmer, B. Franklin. 1862.
Parry, Charles T. 1864.
Purves, Alexander. 1875–1876.
Pemberton, Henry, Jr. 1891 to present time.
Pettit, Horace. 1894 to present time.
Paul, Lawrence T. 1895 to present time.

Ronaldson, James. 1824–1841.
Ramage, Adam. 1824–1832.
Rust, James I. 1824.
Richardson, John. 1825.
Rush, William. 1825.
Ralston, Ashbel G. 1825–1830.
Riehle, Henry J. 1826–1827.
Robbins, Samuel J. 1827–1833.
Rowland, William. 1828.
Roberts, Algernon S. 1828–1829.
Rowland, Jr., James. 1829–1830.
Reeves, Benjamin. 1829–1837.
Richards, Mark. 1831.
Reed, William B. 1832–1836.
Rogers, Henry D. 1838–1843.
Roberts, Solomon W. 1842–1853.
Rogers, Evans. 1854–1863.
Rogers, Fairman. 1864–1866.
Roberts, Percival. 1864–1868.
Reeves, Samuel J. 1864.
Rice, John. 1866–1867.
Rogers, Robert E. 1867–1878.
Rand, Theodore D. 1874 to present time.
Ronaldson, Charles E. 1885–1893.
Reeves, Stacy. 1889 to present time.

Strickland, William. 1824–1826–1828.
Seiper, Thomas. 1824.
Struthers, John. 1827–1849.
Schreiner, Joseph H. 1827–1832.
Souder, Jacob. 1828.
Stevenson, William, Jr. 1828.
Scattergood, Thomas. 1829–1834.
Say, Benjamin. 1832–1833.
Shinn, Earle. 1836–1837.
Stewart, Thomas S. 1842–1850 and 1852–1863.
Saxton, Joseph. 1842–1844.
Savery, Peleg B. 1851–1852.
Smith, Charles E. 1852–1855.
Sellers, William. 1857–1861 and 1864–1892.
Sellers, Coleman. 1862 to present time.
Sloan, Samuel. 1864.
Sartain, Samuel. 1865 to present time.
Sartain, John. 1877–1879.
Shain, Charles J. 1884–1887.

LIST OF BENEFACTORS.

A list of the benefactors of the Institute would be a long one indeed, were it made to include all who are justly entitled to be so considered. Instead, we have confined it to the enumeration of those who have contributed, by bequest or otherwise, substantial sums of money, or made gifts of substantial value, for the furtherance of its work. So far as has been ascertained by the writer, they embrace the following:—

James Ronaldson—a legacy of $500.

A. Miller—a legacy of $1,819.77.

Algernon S. Roberts—a gift of $800 for the purchase of books.

Barnabas H. Bartol—a gift of $1,000 for the endowment of Scholarships in the Drawing School; also a bequest of $5,000 to the building fund.

Elliott Cresson—a gift of $1,000 for the endowment of a Gold Medal to be awarded for discoveries and inventions of pre-eminent value.

Henry Seybert—a gift of $500 for the purchase of books; also a legacy of $2,000 for the building fund.

Evans Rogers—a legacy of $5,000.

Asa Whitney—a legacy of $500.

Mrs. Bloomfield H. Moore—two gifts aggregating $15,000, constituting the "Bloomfield H. Moore Fund," for the endowment of the library.

Uriah A. Boyden—a gift of $1,000 as a prize for the solution of an important problem in physical science (not yet awarded).

John Lenthall—the gift of his valuable personal library of books and drawings relating to naval architecture and marine engineering.

Joseph Neumann—the bequest of a residuary interest in his estate, value at present not estimated.

John Turner—a bequest, consisting of a percentage of the income of his residuary estate, valued at $50 annually.

Mrs. Wm. B. Rogers—the gift of the valuable library of chemical works belonging to the late Dr. Robt. E. Rogers.

Edward Longstreth—a gift of $1,000 for the endowment of a Silver Medal for inventions and works of a meritorious character.

George S. Pepper—a legacy of 25,000, and an additional interest in his residuary estate, for the endowment fund. (This benefaction has amounted thus far to $34,437.50).

Mrs. Frederic Graff—the gift of a valuable collection of drawings and engravings, belonging to her late husband.

Eugene Nugent—a legacy of $1,000 to the endowment fund,

FORMS OF SUBSCRIPTION AND BEQUEST.

I hereby subscribe to the Endowment Fund of the FRANKLIN INSTI-
TUTE OF THE STATE OF PENNSYLVANIA FOR THE PROMOTION OF THE
MECHANIC ARTS, *the sum of One Hundred Dollars as a Life Member-
ship Fee in said Institute.*

Signed,...

Date,................*Address,*................................

————

I hereby subscribe to the Endowment Fund of the FRANKLIN INSTI-
TUTE OF THE STATE OF PENNSYLVANIA FOR THE PROMOTION OF THE
MECHANIC ARTS, *the sum of One Thousand Dollars as a Permanent
Membership Fee in said Institute transferable by will or otherwise.*

Signed,...

Date,................*Address,*................................

————

I hereby subscribe to the FRANKLIN INSTITUTE OF THE STATE OF
PENNSYLVANIA FOR THE PROMOTION OF THE MECHANIC ARTS, *the sum
of*................................*Dollars, to be applied to the
Endowment Fund of the* $\left\{ \begin{matrix} Library \\ Journal \end{matrix} \right\}$ *of said Institute.*

Signed,...

Date,................*Address,*................................

————

I hereby give and bequeath to the FRANKLIN INSTITUTE OF THE
STATE OF PENNSYLVANIA FOR THE PROMOTION OF THE MECHANIC
ARTS, *the sum of*......................*Dollars, to be applied to the
Endowment Fund of said Institute.*

By the several Sections of Article I, of the by-laws of the Institute, it is directed *that all real and personal property of the Institute, which may be acquired by voluntary subscription or devise, bequest or donation,* unless the donors shall expressly provide to the contrary, *shall be taken as acquired upon the condition that the same shall be vested in a Board of Trustees, who shall hold the same in trust for the purposes designated by the donors,* and who are required to keep the principal of these subscriptions, bequests, etc., safely invested, and, from time to time, to pay over the net income derived therefrom to the Board of Managers, to be applied by the Board to the specific purposes named by the donors, or to the general uses of the Institute.